THOUSANDS

A church is born in the Indonesian rainforest

as told to Stewart Dinnen
& Glenn Myers

ISBN 978-0-900828-88-1
10 9 8 7 6 5 4 3 2 1
Published in 2010 by WEC Publications

WEC International, Bulstrode, Oxford Road, Gerrards Cross,
Buckinghamshire SL9 8SZ, England, Great Britain
www.wec-int.org.uk

Typeset by WEC Publications
Cover design by Chris Lawrence
Printed and bound by Lightning Source

British Library Cataloguing in Publication data.
A catalogue record for this book is available from the British Library.

DEDICATION

To that wonderful band of dedicated faithful intercessors (some now in glory), we dedicate this book. Their prayers have had an impact which only eternity will disclose.

Annette Rattray

THANKS

Stewart Dinnen conceived this book, interviewed Bruce and Annette at length, collected testimonies from their co-workers, and produced a first draft of their story.

Bruce and Annette opened their home to me in the final months of Bruce's life and gave me the unforgettable privilege of hearing their stories. Annette and I subsequently worked on the draft to bring it to this final form.

Colleagues and family members gave help and support in various ways. Many thanks to you all.

Bruce used the Authorized Version (KJV) of the Bible in his early life. For clarity, we've used Bible quotations from the NIV unless stated.

Glenn Myers

Bruce on the farm in North-West Tasmania with his father Warren

Bruce, Annette, Paul and Simon Rattray in 1978

AUSTRALIA

1

One day in 1955 two young men were walking down a street in the blustery seaside town of Devonport, on Tasmania's north coast. One – tall, solidly built, with an easy loping stride and a large face – was a Australian Rules football player, Bruce Rattray. Compared to him, the other man looked small.

The two men were walking in silence, the wind flapping their baggy trousers.

'Bruce, I want to ask you a question ... a very important question.'

Bruce glanced down at him. 'Well, go ahead.'

'Bruce, why don't you give your life to Jesus Christ?'

Bruce stopped. *What a funny question.*

'I don't know,' he replied slowly. 'I guess I never thought much about it.'

If I did that – the thought occurred to Bruce – *it would have to be the whole thing. Jesus Christ would have to be literally in control of my whole life.*

The other man did not seem to have anything else to say and after a moment, they both walked on again.

The conversation had taken perhaps ten seconds, but Bruce was never quite the same afterwards. Something had tugged at his heart.

Religion for Robert Bruce Rattray had so far meant nothing more than ancient Anglican vicars filling an hour at school with Religious Instruction classes. This was a total waste of time for someone like Bruce, a regular truant and a complete rascal. Yet, according to a school friend, he was never mean or unkind.

His mum had often ended the day by saying, 'well, he's survived another one.' If his dad had whacked him for no good reason and Bruce had complained, his dad would point out that Bruce was bound to deserve it sooner or later, so getting it early didn't matter all that much.

Bruce was of farming stock. He was brought up with people who, after a hard week running a farm, would play Aussie Rules football – probably the most physical and savage of all the oval-ball games – for fun. In the summers they played cricket. They also raced horses and buggies and held wood-chopping contests.

Twenty-one-year-old Bruce had so excelled at all of these, and especially at amateur football, that the local Aussie Rules team in Devonport had started paying him board and lodging, so that he could train professionally.

After every match a panel of judges awarded points to the three best players, and Bruce was frequently named the best. With scouts from the mainland interested, he should have felt glad to be alive – an athletic young man in the world's most obsessively sport-mad country, the riches of professional football beckoning.

The trouble was, he didn't. He couldn't put his finger on why, but he didn't feel totally at home among his fellow Aussie Rules friends and team-mates. When he went with them for a drink, or to see a film, Bruce felt he was putting on an act. And they were doing the same – pretending. *There's got to be more to life than this*, he thought more than once, but the emptiness grew and took hold.

Now buzzing away in his mind was this extra thought: *If I ever gave my life to Jesus Christ, it would have to be the whole thing. Jesus Christ would have to be literally in control of my whole life.* It wasn't a happy thought, and Bruce kept swatting it away, but it kept coming back.

At the end of the season he was voted best player in the league. All Bruce could feel was dissatisfaction shrouding his heart and the looming, uncomfortable presence of Jesus Christ behind him, always just out of reach.

2

Two years later, Bruce was at home on their farm in a remote spot in North-West Tasmania. The phone rang. Bruce's father, Warren, a man built on the same lines as his son except that he was even bigger and squarer, came into the kitchen and wrapped his huge hand around the phone.

'Yes, doctor,' Bruce heard him say, with an unusual hush in his voice, as if he were listening very carefully. 'I'll come straight away.'

'Garth's suddenly got a lot worse,' Warren said quickly. 'I'm going to have to drive down and see him.'

Garth was Bruce's younger brother who in his early teens had been as athletic as Bruce and perhaps even more skilful. He had once been picked to represent Tasmania at the Junior Aussie Rules Football Carnival in Brisbane. His recent years had been dominated by liver disease. While Bruce had spent the football season playing in Devonport, Garth was in and out of hospital, gaunt, weak and yellow.

Bruce suddenly felt an enormous sense of urgency hit him, out of nowhere. It was overwhelming. 'Dad! I've got to go with you!'

'Well who's going to look after the cows?' snapped Warren. They were milking around 90 cows, with Bruce the leading hand.

'Dad, I don't know what we'll do, but I've got to go with you.'

They talked about it and decided that Warren would drive the 150 km to Launceston in the family car, while Bruce took Garth's little Austin A30. Then he could see Garth and get back quickly to the farm.

They arrived mid-afternoon. Bruce parked more quickly than his father, strode into the hospital, made a few enquiries, and found Garth's room, without waiting for his dad. He pushed through the door and they greeted each other.

Bruce could see in Garth's yellow-tinged eyes that Garth was dying. Up till now, Bruce had never really accepted that Garth's liver disease was going to kill him. It was truly shocking looking at him now, jaundiced and bone-thin.

They had been very close. They loved each other. They'd never had a serious fight. They'd played football and cricket together and together competed in wood-chopping competitions. Seeing him now, Bruce hardly knew what to say.

He cast around for a bit then started to exchange some football gossip. Even as he talked on, Bruce hated himself. *All I can talk about is my football and myself. My brother is dying, and I love him, and I can't say anything to comfort him, not really comfort him. I don't have anything to give him.*

Bruce didn't go home the next day. The rest of the family gathered, taking turns to sit by Garth's bed. Step by step, they watched his body shut down. He slipped into a coma. His skin turned from yellow to grey.

One night (Bruce found out later), Warren was taking his turn at Garth's bedside. He wasn't a religious man. But in the secrecy of the darkened room, with no-one watching, he slipped off his chair and knelt by his son's bed.

'Please heal my son,' he whispered to God. 'And I will follow you forever.'

In the silence, Warren was utterly surprised when God answered back. 'How many times have you prayed that? How many times has he recovered? And how many times have you then turned your back on me again?'

In the darkness, Garth was sleeping peacefully.

After some moments, still kneeling and brooding, and now blinking back the tears, Warren whispered slowly: 'All right. All right, Lord. If you give my son back, I'm yours. If you take my son, I'm yours. Either way, I'm yours.'

The next day, Garth died.

Bruce never forgot that nightmare day – watching his tough Australian farmer father, his cheeks wet, running his fingers through Garth's curly dark hair. His father then breaking the news to his mum with the words, 'All his troubles are over'.

Finally, a distant relative who was a lay preacher reading something and praying. As this man prayed, something impressed Bruce deeply. *This man*, he thought, *really knows God.*

Bruce had to organize the funeral. He could hardly imagine a job he wanted less. Yet when it came to it, something happened that gave him a strange sense of euphoria. As he took one last look at Garth's face before the coffin lid was shut, words rolled into Bruce's head:

Where, O death is your victory?
Where, O death is your sting?

He had only the faintest idea that they might be from the Bible. (The verse is 1 Corinthians 15:55.) But they struck a chord. Garth, he knew, had made a Christian commitment during one of his previous hospital stays, through the influence of a Salvation Army chaplain. Bruce had noticed the difference in his brother without exactly knowing why or how he had changed.

When they got into the taxi to go to the cemetery, the driver said, 'Bad luck, mate: he was only young too.'

'No, not bad luck,' Bruce gabbled back, surprising himself. 'He's with the Lord! Isn't that wonderful?'

Little got done after they returned. Bruce's mother withdrew into a deep grief. Warren was walking around dazed and weeping. For Bruce, his brother's death had brought all his vague feelings over the past couple of years to a sharp point.

He rooted through the family's thin collection of religious books: a Book of Mormon, which he quickly discarded as useless; a Bible, which he leafed through randomly, reading passages, understanding little. Then he found this verse: *'The kingdom of heaven suffereth violence and the violent take it by force'* (Matthew 11:12, KJV).

He didn't know what it meant. He knew that he didn't have the kingdom of heaven – whatever it was – but if it could be taken by force, well, he, Bruce, was going to take it.

He became obsessive, determined to meet with God. When he got up in the morning he asked himself, *'I wonder if I'll find God today?'* When night came, and he hadn't 'found God', he went to bed thinking, *'Perhaps I'll find him tomorrow'*. He didn't want to eat.

A few days after the funeral, Bruce was lying on his bed in the room he had shared with Garth, while Warren was lying on Garth's old bed.

'Do you know what Garth said to me a few days before he died?' said Warren, looking up at the ceiling and crying. 'He said, "Dad, you can live without Jesus Christ, but you can't die without him!" How about that? He's right too!'

Later on, after listening to his dad cry for a long time, Bruce said, 'Dad! No amount of tears is going to bring Garth back again.'

Warren looked across at him, eyes still full of tears.

'Bruce, I'm not weeping because my son has died. I'm weeping because of what my sin has done to God.' In losing his own son, Warren had caught a glimpse of what it had cost the Father to give up His own Son.

Another day, some people came to visit, friends of the Christian cousins in Launceston. They tried to explain the gospel, but it didn't seem to help. They gave Bruce things to read, but they didn't help either. If anything, God seemed to be slipping further away. A great sense of doom had begun to hang over Bruce. He realized that God was perfectly within his rights to send him to Hell, and that if he did, Bruce could have no complaint.

So there was no escape. Bruce worked it out: he could probably behave pretty well by stern self-discipline and great effort. Maybe, he felt, he could even tame his tongue. But his thoughts, his anger – it was impossible. Yet at the same time as this sense of gloom and condemnation overshadowed him, he couldn't escape the sense that somehow out there, a loving God was urging him on.

It got too much. A few weeks after Garth's funeral, Bruce said to himself, *'I'm going to settle this.'* He walked into his bedroom, closed the door deliberately, knelt down by the bed, and poured out his heart to God.

'Oh God! What must I do?'

In the silence, he saw a brief vision of Jesus on the cross.

'You don't have to do anything.' The words fell quietly into his spirit. *'He already did it all, when he died for you.'*

You don't have to do anything. He already did it all, when he died for you. With that one sentence, Bruce found that the burden that had been crushing him fell away.

When he got up from his knees, it had gone. He felt around in his mind for it, but it wasn't there. In its place was something steady and happy – heart-contact with God. Unbelievable! Inside, he was clean – cleansed.

He raced out of the bedroom.

'Mum! I've found the Lord!'

'Oh. That's nice for you, Bruce,' she said, going back to the vegetables she was unloading in the kitchen. Outside the house, the district grocer in his van was just about to leave.

Bruce strode out. 'Pat, I've got something to tell you, something wonderful!'

'You look pretty pleased about it!' said the grocer, smiling.

'Pat, I just found the Lord in there, kneeling by my bed! I'm saved, Pat! Isn't that marvellous?'

A cloud passed over the grocer's face. Without a word he slammed the sides of his van down as quickly as he could and took off in a cloud of dust.

3

Each new day took the family only a tiny step further from Garth's loss, which still spread itself behind them like a storm-front, filling half the sky. At the same time, Warren and Bruce began to get used to the new idea of knowing God. One of Bruce's sisters had also found peace with God. Life began to stir again. Bruce and Warren resumed some of the farm work, enjoying the routine and the manual labour.

About the first Sunday after Bruce became a Christian, he and Warren were each working their way through their usual plateful of bacon and eggs, chops and sausages, loading the food from plate to mouth like men stocking a warehouse. (Their appetites had returned with their faith.) They were talking about baling hay from a paddock they had mown before Garth's death. Fresh grass was growing up, making it difficult to bale.

'You know,' said Warren, after gulping down a big draught of tea. 'We should go to church today but that paddock of hay is going to be spoiled if we don't bale it.'

'You want me to bale it then?'

'Yes.'

A bit reluctantly, Bruce got out the tractor and started the baling. Hardly five minutes into the job, he heard a huge *clunk*, so he put the engine into neutral, jumped down, looked at the baler and saw the universal joint sheared. With a grunt of disapproval he went back to the tractor and cut the engine. He would have to get the car out and drive into Smithton to buy a new part.

A couple of hours later, they finally finished fitting the new part, and were hot and greasy. Bruce climbed into the tractor, started the engine up again, and Warren watched him as he set off across the paddock. The baler ran fine for a few dozen yards and then *clunk*.

'What was that?' He cut the engine a second time, jumped down, took a look.

'I don't believe it!' Same joint, same total wreck, two or three more wasted hours to fix it.

'Dad,' said Bruce, smiling a little, 'you know, I don't think the Lord wants us to cut this field today.'

4

A few weeks later, Bruce played a game of cricket for his local team. It was an away match, and afterwards it was normal to stop off in a bar on the way back. Bruce had given up drinking: he never had liked it all that much and had decided to make a clean break.

He was driving a couple of team-mates and hoped just to take them quietly home, but as they passed the pub, one of them shouted out, 'Hey! Aren't you going to go in?'

He pulled over. *No way am I'm going to get out of this one*, Bruce thought. He parked and as they made their way to the bar, Bruce noticed that the entire team was there.

'What'll you have, Bruce?' someone asked.

'Er – a lemonade and raspberry please.'

'Hey – what's the matter? You not feeling well?'

Part of Bruce just wanted to say 'yeah'. But then the Aussie Rules player in him took over. He cleared his throat.

'Fellas,' he said loudly. 'Fellas, I've got something to say.'

Everyone looked up. The whole hotel went silent, apart from the glug-glug-glug of the bartender adding lemonade to the raspberry juice. Bruce noticed a certain slackness in his knees, not something he usually felt, even when half a dozen Aussie Rules players were about to jump on him and leave studmarks.

He didn't know what words to use. 'Fellas, last week on the farm I gave my life to the Lord.' His mouth was dry. He could have really used the lemonade. 'I promised the Lord I wouldn't drink again and that's why I'm not drinking today.'

Men started looking at their boots, at the ceiling, into their beer, inspecting the beer-mats. One or two were looking right at him, bewildered looks on their faces. One person called out, 'I wish I had your faith!' Another swore. 'You've become one of those religious fanatics, have you?'

Bruce's two farmer friends got back into the car with him for the journey back. For a long half-hour Bruce drove, hearing nothing but the whine of Garth's old Austin A30, the person next to him looking straight forward, the eyes of the person in the back seat boring into him.

5

The change in Warren Rattray was even more drastic. A life that had been entirely centred on Warren Rattray became entirely centred on Jesus Christ. He loved Christ with a passion. Strong, irascible, controlling, Warren brought his personality along into his new lifestyle.

He became a completely outspoken evangelist, arguing publicly and loudly with anyone who contradicted him, unafraid of making a scene, completely careless of criticism. He had not yet learnt the scriptures that talked about '*a time to be silent and a time to speak*' (Ecclesiastes 3:7) and that when you do speak, do so with '*gentleness and respect*' (1 Peter 3:15).

Within a few months of his conversion, Warren had come across a book called *Rees Howells – Intercessor*, the famous story of the extraordinary prayer life of a former Welsh miner. Rees

Howells had been as rough and stubborn as Warren himself. The book told how special seasons of prayer for Rees Howells coincided with remarkable turning points in the Second World War.

When the weather became extraordinarily calm for the Dunkirk evacuation, when Goering called off an air attack on Britain, not knowing that the RAF had no fighters left in reserve, Rees Howells was praying for a great deliverance. When Hitler unexpectedly turned towards Russia, when Montgomery defeated the Afrika Korps, Rees Howells was praying and following the events in the newspapers – and sometimes predicting the outcome by faith. The book absolutely fascinated Warren Rattray. He read it over and over. He told Bruce that many times he had to put the book aside and get down onto the floor and cry out to God to give him a prayer life like that.

If Warren's personality was not perhaps best suited to evangelism it was entirely suited, as the Holy Spirit shaped and gifted him, to an extreme striving with God through prayer. Warren became a soldier who, once given orders by his Commanding Officer to trust God for a certain thing, would stay in the prayer trenches all day and all night.

It was not unusual for Warren to sit down for the evening meal with the family and say, 'Let's give thanks for the food.'

He would start off, 'Lord, we thank you …' but then tears would fill his eyes and he would get up from the table, looking uncharacteristically sheepish, and hurry to the bedroom. The family would hear him sobbing and groaning and calling out to God. Hours after they'd finished the meal, he would emerge, face filled with joy.

The farm work was still languishing. Bruce and Warren were doing only the essentials and spending a lot of time reading, praying, discussing what they found in their Bibles, enjoying a kind of honeymoon of God's love.

One time Warren called Bruce up from the paddock.

'Bruce! Quick!' Bruce ran in.

'What is it? What's the matter?'

'Aw, there were some angels here, but they've gone now.'

A couple of months after Garth's death, Bruce was ambling back after working in the paddock when he saw his dad in the far distance, standing by the big milk vat, looking like he was about to draw out a bucketful of milk to feed the pigs. He was standing very still. As Bruce watched, he noticed Warren wasn't moving – he just stood by the milk vat, rigid, upright.

Maybe he's having a heart attack. As Bruce hurried nearer, squelching through the mud, he could hear Warren weeping.

'Dad! Dad! What's wrong?'

'Oh, it's your mum.'

'What do you mean? Has something happened to Mum?'

'No, no. She's not saved. I'm praying for her.'

Bruce went back to his work. A long time later he returned and there was Warren still standing by the milk vat. This time his face was shining.

'Dad?'

'You don't need to pray any more. I've prayed.'

That night, Bruce's mother made her peace with God.

6

Around this time, Bruce became very struck by a Bible verse:

'You are not your own; you were bought with a price; therefore honour God with your body' (1 Corinthians 6:19-20).

He began to pray daily: 'Lord, I belong to you. I will go to any place, to any people, at any time, to bring them the gospel. All I ask is that you make it so clear that I can never doubt it.'

Seeing the way he was leaning, Bruce's pastor, Ken Finger advised him to do training at a Bible college. Bruce applied, and in January 1958 he left Tasmania for Melbourne Bible Institute (now called the Bible College of Victoria). MBI was intended to take zealous young men and women and give them a good grounding in the Bible and coaching in ministry skills.

It came like a slap of cold water to Bruce. Raw and belligerent, he argued long and loud with some fellow students, all of them striving to be first and right.

For Bruce this was totally unexpected, and completely depressing. He found his joy and excitement at being a Christian vanishing down some sort of plughole.

His response to all this defined how he approached problems ever afterwards. He took off to a quiet room (actually the broom cupboard) and long after the official lights-out, he began to pray and seek answers from God. He was going to do this until God answered him definitively. He went on week after week.

He began to cry out to God for the power of the Holy Spirit to live and speak well. As the weeks passed, God led him to pray prayers that defined him for the rest of his life.

'Lord, I would rather be a doorkeeper in the house of God than dwell in the tents of wickedness.'

'Lord, I want so to preach the gospel that people are converted.'

'Lord, make my life like broken bread and poured out wine that Christ's life in me may feed many.'

One day Bruce was preparing a talk in his room. Another student was working quietly nearby. Bruce was reading the passage at the very end of John's gospel, when the risen Jesus took Peter for a lakeside walk, and began untangling that apostle's confusion of passion, ambition and failure.

'Peter, do you love me more than these?'

In the quiet room, the question drilled into Bruce's heart, as if Jesus was asking Bruce,

Do you love me more than your parents? 'Yes, Lord, I do.'

More than your ambitions? 'Yes, Lord, I do.'

More than your reputation? 'Yes.'

More than all your possessions? 'Yes, Lord, I do.'

More than your car? Bruce smiled to himself. 'Yes Lord, I do. I do. I'd gladly leave them all for you.'

It was as if the Lord were asking Bruce, *Do you love me, not for what I did for you, just for who I am? Do you love me?*

'Yes, Lord, I do.'

And then Jesus asked Peter a third time, *'Simon son of Jonah, do you love me?'*

In the story, Peter is grieved because Jesus asked him a third time; and Bruce was grieved too. 'Lord, you know all things. You know that I love you. You know.'

It was a holy moment, though the student across the room

from Bruce didn't seem to notice. 'You know that I love you,' he told Jesus. 'And I know that you know. I know that I love you supremely and I know that you know.'

Before the moment ended, Jesus said quietly to Bruce's heart: *I fill you with my Spirit! Now go and preach!*

7

That weekend Bruce was booked to preach at a church called Gardner Congregational Church because the pastor was sick.

Bruce had prepared a startling sermon out of a text in Hebrews, *'Without holiness no-one will see the Lord'* (Hebrews 12:14). He had been reading the American revivalist Charles Finney who stressed the absolute importance of bringing people to a point where they knew that outside of Christ, no-one could stand before a holy God.

He felt so full of his message, he could hardly wait for the preliminaries to be over before he got to the pulpit. As he enlarged on his theme, he felt a power he had never known before. One man got up, stormed out of the church, slamming the door. Bruce finished his message and invited anyone who was not ready to meet God to stay behind. Then he announced the final hymn.

There was a longer-than-usual pause. Bruce looked over at the organist and saw her, head in hands, weeping quietly.

What have I done? he thought.

Eventually she pulled herself together and they cranked their way through the last hymn. He made his way to the door to meet people on the way out, but no-one moved.

What do I do now? Bruce wondered.

He had told them he would talk to them individually, so he set off down the aisle again and worked his way back through the congregation, urging them to keep seeking God until they really knew that they had truly found him.

A love relationship with Jesus, overflowing into a passion for people to find Christ and his salvation: this became what Bruce was all about, and the legacy of his two years at Bible College.

'I have only one string on my fiddle,' he often said, 'and I'll play it till I die.'

8

Bruce was still repeating vows to the Lord, so almost every day he was praying some of them, including,

'Lord, I will go to any people, anywhere, at any time. All I ask is that you show me so clearly that I can never doubt it.'

And, 'Lord, I won't look at a girl until you show me the one of your choice.'

Bruce's parents had moved to the city of Launceston, and now worshipped at a church called Elphin Road Baptist Church. When he was home, Bruce joined them.

One night in June 1959, an English missionary came to speak about his work in Sabah, in the Malaysian part of the jungle island of Borneo. He showed slides of the Dayak people he worked among – small, shy forest people who lived communally in rickety-looking longhouses deep in the jungle, pigs rooting about for scraps underneath.

After Bruce got home, he shut himself in his room, with the black-and-white jungle pictures still roosting in his mind. He started praying, trying to remember the stories and people that the missionary had described. As he prayed, though, he didn't feel he was particularly getting anywhere, and he seemed to sense the Lord saying, *Keep quiet. I've something to say to you.*

The impression came into his mind, *read Deuteronomy.* Puzzled, Bruce picked up his Bible and checked through it. Deuteronomy has 32 chapters. *This is going to be a long night,* he thought.

He started at chapter one and came to verse 8: *'Behold I have set the land before you'* (KJV).

'That's it' said Bruce. Somehow that verse grabbed his heart, as if God himself were speaking through it. He never asked God again where he ought to serve. Instead, he returned to MBI, praising God for the peace and confidence in his heart.

The vow about a wife, however, he still kept repeating nearly every day.

9

Sometime in the next few months (Bruce heard this much later), his sister Judy came to visit her parents in Launceston. She worshipped with them at the Baptist Church. On the Sunday night, Warren also gave a young trainee midwife a ride home from church, dropping her off at the hospital.

'Who's that beautiful girl?' asked Judy, after they drove out of the hospital car park.

'That girl – Anne?' said Warren, 'Oh, that's Bruce's wife.'

'What did you say?'

'That's the girl Bruce is going to marry.'

'Dad. You cannot –'

'I'm telling you. That's her all right.'

'Dad! That is just –'

'You wait and see. That's her. I know.'

As his time at MBI was coming to an end, Bruce was working out the next stage in his preparation for Borneo, and intended applying for a course in linguistics. One morning, he opened a letter from his dad. With his usual directness Warren wrote, 'I think the Lord is going to call you back to the farm for a time.' Warren had the idea that Bruce could go to work a farm he had bought in Bridgenorth, near Launceston.

Later that day, as Bruce again sought God through prayer and Bible reading, he sensed God speaking to him through another Bible verse, Habakkuk 2:3, *'The vision is yet for an appointed time. Though it tarry, wait for it because in the end it shall speak and not lie'* (KJV).

So reluctantly, instead of going on to further training, he moved back home.

On the final Sunday of 1959, Bruce was back at Elphin Road Baptist Church, having now graduated from MBI. He noticed a young woman sitting in front of him.

She looks nice, he thought. Later in the service she got up to sing a solo. She was small, with long blonde curly hair.

She sang a wonderful consecration hymn. That night, having hardly spoken to her – her name was Annette – Bruce asked the Lord, 'Is she the one?'

In his heart he sensed the Lord's clear reply, *Yes she is.*

10

When Bruce Rattray fell in love, it was like everything else with him – simple, wholehearted, certain.

He looked out for Annette at every possible church meeting, cornering her by the tea urn. Dating was not straightforward in the conservative world of backwoods Tasmania where Bruce came from, and in any case he felt rather awkward in the presence of girls. His sister Judy was again visiting, so he enlisted her help and a friendship began – based, they soon found, on a shared love for Jesus and a common desire to serve him overseas.

After that, Annette started to come over to the Rattray household fairly often, despite the dangerously robust hospitality. A warm handshake from Warren could leave her painfully untangling her fingers. Warren called her a 'poor doer', like a sickly calf, because she hardly ate anything, according to him. Once (fortunately for Annette, only once) he slapped her playfully on the back and knocked her off her feet.

Bruce, meanwhile, was utterly besotted with this beautiful

girl. As soon as he could, he sat her down and told her she was going to be his wife and they were going to serve God together.

'Isn't it wonderful?' He said.

To his total and utter surprise, Annette didn't seem to think it was so wonderful at all.

Annette's midwifery course finished. She flew home to Brisbane, half a continent away. Bruce took her to the airport and they said a rather quiet farewell, Annette still carefully placing herself outside of a commitment to Bruce.

He watched the plane clatter into the sky, and again felt a word from God enter his head. He hardly recognized it as scripture at all, though he eventually found it in the Bible. He didn't know what it meant, either:

I will give you the treasures of darkness (Isaiah 45:3).

11

Bruce threw himself into fixing up the Bridgenorth farm. Except for trips back to Launceston or to church, Bruce was completely on his own. It was strange: from the buzz of his ministry in Melbourne, he was left just with sheep, fields, and utter solitude. No ministry, no company, no complications, nothing to distract. He loved it.

At the time, some of Tasmania's small evangelical Christian community was tearing itself into shreds over theological controversy. Bruce's church itself split. Launceston had its own missionary training college run by a large agency called WEC International, and it too had split, the principal and most of the students walking out to found their own institution.

In Bridgenorth, despairing over the wreckage, Bruce set himself on the most determined and sustained time of seeking the Lord he had ever known. He would do his farm work, fix his evening meal, and then read his Bible and pray long into the Tasmanian winter night.

He started with the aim of sorting out what the Bible itself said about the controversy. He sometimes read his Bible and prayed from six in the evening until one in the morning. Months passed, with Bruce farming by day and devoting all his spare time to seeking God. He would go to bed, mind and heart full of scripture, and wake up with an overwhelming sense of the Lord's presence. More than once he spent a whole day ploughing a paddock and hardly noticed the day passing as he rolled and unrolled the great truths of scripture in his mind.

One day, he was baling hay. Warren had just dropped him off at the farm. Suddenly Bruce felt an overpowering urge to pray. The urge was so intense and overwhelming he stopped the tractor and started walking towards the farmhouse. He walked faster and finally sprinted to get inside, close the door, get on the floor, and cry out to God. He didn't know what it was all about, this sudden call to God's side. Had his dad had a car crash on the road back to Launceston?

As he lay there, groaning with the sense of God's Spirit on him, Bruce felt God showing him that the extreme Reformed view, to which the Christians who were involved were having to agree as a sign of their orthodoxy, was all wrong in its spirit

– misrepresenting God, extinguishing zeal for lost people, tying Christians down rather than freeing them up.

Annette, up in Brisbane, managed what few Aussie Rules players and no large trees had ever done: she refused to be moved by Bruce Rattray. She was not going to commit herself to Bruce until she knew for herself, from God, that this was God's will. She might be smaller than him – she was actually half his weight – but she could be just as tough.

12

Bruce's appetite for God kept growing. And he still couldn't escape a nagging feeling of restlessness, frustration, and failure. All the blessing he was drinking in seemed to make it rise to the surface. He knew about confession and forgiveness, how he could bring to Christ his wrong doing or wrong thinking, be forgiven, and start again. But he was aware of a deep lack of spiritual resources.

Was life just going to be a round of failing, confessing, being forgiven, starting again? Or were there resources somehow in God that dealt with the power of sin as well as with the guilt of sin? The solitude and the intense search for truth only highlighted this great blot on his personal landscape.

He knew about forgiveness. He knew what it was to have a heart full of love for Christ. But where was the power to live consistently? The New Testament talks about victory, not just forgiveness. Deep within, Bruce knew he had not accessed these spiritual resources. He could echo Romans 7:22-23:

'For in my inner being I delight in God's law; but I see another law at work in the members of my body, waging war against the law of my mind and making me a prisoner of the law of sin at work within my members.'

Or more simply,

'What a wretched man I am! Who will rescue me from this body of death?' (verse 24).

Like many believers before and since, he was stuck in his Christian experience at the end of Romans chapter 7, unable honestly to make the affirmation in Romans chapter 8:

'... through Christ Jesus the law of the Spirit of life set me free from the law of sin and death.'

He started devouring some of the books from the so-called Holiness Movement within evangelicalism: titles like *In Christ* by A J Gordon, *Born Crucified* by L E Maxwell, *The Normal Christian Life* by Watchman Nee, and *Bone of His Bone* by F J Huegel.

All these books – to his intense irritation – smugly testified to some experience or some kind of realization, some realm of faith or *something* that seemed to deal directly with his problem. But they didn't solve it. He tried every way he knew to get into this experience and ended up flinging *The Normal Christian Life* across the room.

Finding these spiritual self-help books little help, he took a Bible prayer and started praying that, turning it over and over before God:

'I keep asking that the God of our Lord Jesus Christ, the glorious

Father, may give you the Spirit of wisdom and revelation, so that you may know him better. I pray also that the eyes of your heart may be enlightened in order that you may know the hope to which he has called you, the riches of his glorious inheritance in the saints, and his incomparably great power for us who believe. That power is like the working of his mighty strength, which he exerted in Christ when he raised him from the dead and seated him at his right hand in the heavenly realms, far above all rule and authority, power and dominion, and every title that can be given, not only in the present age but also in the one to come' (Ephesians 1:17-21).

Bruce made this prayer his own, using it like a hand to tug at Christ's robes. 'Enlighten my eyes that I may know.'

One morning after about a week of praying this prayer, Bruce was reading John's account of the crucifixion, death and burial of our Lord.

'Suddenly', Bruce recounted later, 'the Lord asked me a question. *"Did Jesus really die?"* I remembered the terrible scourging, the agony as He hung nailed to that awful cross – the loud cry – the thrust of the Roman spear, the body wrapped in the grave clothes covered with the mixture of myrrh and aloes, and I replied, "Yes, Lord, He surely died."

'Then ever so quietly – it seemed almost as if time stood still – He spoke again just a few words which totally transformed my Christian walk.

'"If He died, then you died, for you were in Him when He died!"

'Then I understood! Everything was in Christ and I was in Christ! I did not have to strive to become a branch of the Vine. I was already a part of the Vine.

'If I had been crucified with Christ, I had also been buried with Him – if I had been buried with Him then I had also been raised with Him and if I had been raised with Him then I was also seated with Him. This meant that I was now a partaker of His victory over the world, the flesh and the Devil. I was actually reigning with Christ.'

At that point, the holiness books (as well as much of the New Testament) began to make sense, particularly the Chinese author Watchman Nee's idea of knowing, reckoning, and then standing in the truth.

This truth of union with Christ did not mean Bruce never sinned again. What it did mean was a certainty and an easy freedom about his life and ministry from then on. He knew who and what he was. Christian living was about applying what was true, not trying to make something true that wasn't true: *'Count yourselves dead to sin but alive to God in Christ Jesus'* (Romans 6:11).

This truth of union with Christ dominated Bruce's ministry ever afterwards – just as it predominated in the Apostle Paul's letters, with his repetition in the epistles of the phrases 'in Him', 'in Christ', 'with Him', 'together with Him'.

It also dominated his letters to Annette, which were averaging about twenty pages a week at this point.

Bruce went on to learn more. He began to see the enormity of what happened at the resurrection: Christ is raised far above all powers and principalities in the heavenly realms; not just raised above them, but leading them captive, having bound them up, as if with a great chain. And Bruce – like all Christians – was in Christ, participating in all this.

These truths were liberating, and Bruce used them all his life, in the same way a workman uses his tools.

13

Bruce continued to preach to great effect. His preaching was simple, plain, to the point. Of all the things he hated, nominal Christianity was the worst. Time and again he sought to make sure that people in the congregation had clearly met Christ and knew his forgiveness; not just vaguely gone along with things and hoped for the best. He wanted them to be totally sure that their sins were forgiven because they had put their trust in Jesus. He wanted them in the same love relationship he himself enjoyed.

Young people and old in the congregation were being stirred by his ministry, though some were offended at first – he could be very blunt in those early days.

As he preached one Sunday – it was now late 1960 – the congregation included a Scottish couple, Bible teachers called Stewart and Marie Dinnen. Sent by WEC International, they had come to repair the damage done to the mission agency's training college in Launceston.

In Scotland, the Dinnens had pioneered radical experiments for training Christian workers. For a time they sent students out on preaching tours, which the students had to organize as they went along. They were given a pound sterling to start with, were not allowed to ask for money and they had to give the pound back at the end.

As Bruce shared what he was discovering about union with Christ and spiritual authority in Christ's name, Stewart started to invite Bruce to speak at meetings organized by the college. Sometimes – Bruce claimed much later – Stewart would organize further meetings to help straighten out the confusion that Bruce left behind. It was one of Stewart's gifts to be able to work with raw, gifted people.

Annette left Brisbane and entered the Melbourne Bible Institute. She was geographically nearer, but still frustratingly uncertain about Bruce and her future. Then in their two rooms, in Melbourne and Bridgenorth, separated by the Bass Strait, two things happened to Bruce and Annette at almost the same time.

In Bridgenorth Bruce was trying to construct some theological way of understanding what was happening – it might be God's will, but if she doesn't see it, maybe it won't happen – when he decided to go over again all the promises that he felt God had made to him about Annette.

They were there in his Bible, way-marks of the Spirit's dealings. He couldn't give them up. 'Lord,' he said, 'you have promised it and I am going to believe it. You are going to call Annette to Borneo, and she is going to become my wife.'

In Melbourne, Annette found herself being humbled and broken as she encountered God in a new way. The major issues about Bruce and where she should serve – issues that would determine all of her future – were now laid aside as she just surrendered herself afresh to God.

She made Romans 12:1 – *'Therefore, I urge you, brothers, in view of God's mercy, to offer your bodies as living sacrifices, holy and pleasing to God …'* – her daily *'spiritual act of worship'*, a practice that became a life-long holy ritual.

Verse 2 also became a daily prayer and resolution: *'Do not conform any longer to the pattern of this world, but be transformed by the renewing of your mind.'* And there was a lot of transforming to do, she found! The second half of that verse says: *'Then you will be able to test and approve what God's will is – his good, pleasing and perfect will.'*

The barriers that had kept her from knowing God's will came tumbling down and Annette sensed an increasing peace and clarity about Bruce. She also began to grasp the truth of her union with Christ that Bruce was so passionately writing to her about.

Right at this time, MBI had two unusual missionary visitors within a few weeks of each other: Isabel Stephenson and Percy King. Both spoke of work among Dayaks in Borneo, even though Percy's work with OMF was among Chinese. Nobody had visited MBI to speak about Borneo in the preceding four years; to Annette it was a clear confirmation of God's place of service.

A letter in Annette's neat handwriting fluttered across the Bass Strait, finding its way from Annette's hand to Bruce's. Bruce claimed afterwards he didn't need to open it: he knew what was inside. She was going to marry him, and serve God with him in Borneo.

14

Bruce was finding out more about WEC International. WEC was a pioneering Christian agency set up to establish churches in the neediest, most remote places of the world.

It had been founded by an outstanding sportsman, CT Studd, the best all-round England cricketer of his day. (Studd was at the non-striker's end on the day England lost to Australia for the first time and the bails were cremated to make the 'Ashes'. If he had been facing the bowling during that fateful final over, the whole history of England v. Australia contests would probably have been different! To this day, Studd's name appears on the 'Ashes' urn.)

WEC was a 'faith mission' with strict policies never to appeal for funds. Instead, WEC workers simply prayed and trusted God to provide what was needed: it was good practical experience for trusting God in everything else. If God didn't send money, as sometimes happened, the average WEC worker would usually prefer to go without (or leave the mission) rather than solicit support. If you think WEC tended to attract the more stubborn sort of Christian worker, you'd be right.

WEC was pioneering a work in Borneo, and as the months passed, it became clear to Bruce and Annette that God wanted them to serve in Borneo within this mission. Annette already had close ties to WEC through their Queensland headquarters.

In early 1962 Bruce completed the application process, left the farm, and flew to the WEC headquarters in Sydney to start several months of pre-field orientation and training.

In 1963, Annette also joined WEC and the way was cleared for

Bruce and Annette to be officially engaged. In lieu of a ring, they bought a two-ring Primus stove.

Later in the year, Indonesia refused Bruce's visa, so in April 1964 – the only day in all of his Christian life that Bruce was too excited to read his Bible – they were married by Rev. Gerhard Bargen, the director of WEC Queensland. In June, they applied again for a visa.

Stewart Dinnen had suggested that they return to the WEC training college in Tasmania, where Bruce had earlier looked after the small farm. They could enjoy their early months of married life together, and wait until the Indonesian government decided to let them in. Little did they know how long that would be!

Stewart Dinnen was keen that the MTC modelled a lifestyle as much as passing on information. The staff drew no salary, and staff and students ate, worked, prayed, and played together.

Students quickly learnt about Bruce's enormous drive and energy, by hearing him preach or pray, or watching him playing all positions at once on the volleyball court. In volleyball, it was much safer to play against Bruce rather than alongside him.

As befitted WEC's ethos, MTC was a great school for practical faith. The 'living by faith' principle was a thorough training in learning to walk with God. Once, one of the dairy herd came down with what Bruce recognized as milk fever. It often affects the best milkers in the herd; after calving they get down on the ground and can't get up.

Bruce watched one of his best milking cows struggle like this for three days. On the fourth day he reluctantly got his shotgun and went over to the cow to put her out of her misery. But as he was cocking the gun, she looked up at him, so bright-eyed and full of life that he couldn't do it. He thought for a moment, then walked back over to the college, and fetched Stewart. The two of them – Bruce in his old farm clothes, Stewart dapper as always in collar and tie – stood over the cow, in the dark evening, feeling slightly foolish. They laid their hands on the cow's head.

'You pray,' said Stewart.

'OK,' said Bruce. 'Lord, you know all about this milk fever, and I pray that you would do for this cow whatever most glorifies your name. Amen.'

Bruce opened his eyes and looked down at the cow, which looked hopefully back up at them. Nothing happened. Bruce decided to give it one more day.

Later that evening, as Bruce went out to turn off the irrigation, he ambled over to see the cow. She'd gone. He found her with the rest of the herd, munching on some grass, all trace of milk fever gone.

Another time, they were having a prayer day at the college, and Stewart asked Bruce to share any needs on the farm. Bruce explained that they had lots of grass, and they could do with a few more cows to make the most of it.

'How many exactly?' asked Stewart.

'Well, we could do with two more,' Bruce replied after a thought.

So the staff and students started praying that God would provide two more cows for the farm. After a few people had prayed, they felt no need to continue praying. God had heard, so they went on to another topic.

Later that afternoon, Bruce had to leave the prayer meeting to do the milking. While in the milking shed, he heard a vehicle pull up and a farmer friend, called Noel Flowers, arrived.

They greeted each other and Noel asked, 'Are you having a good year, Bruce?'

'Yes, there's lots of grass.'

'Could you do with two more cows?'

'As a matter of fact we could.'

'Well, I took two to the sale but they didn't go. I don't want to take them home. They're good milking cows, good stock. Could you use them?'

15

A few months later, Bruce was reading his Bible and came across a verse in Revelation (3:8): *'See, I have placed before you an open door that no-one can shut.'*

Again Bruce felt that God was reaffirming that Borneo was the place for them. He thanked God for the fresh reassurance. It would certainly be nice to get their hands on that visa at last.

While they were on holiday celebrating their first wedding anniversary in April 1965, their visa application was turned down again.

On 30 September 1965, seven weeks after the premature birth of their first son, Paul, Bruce felt a strong urge to pray. He stayed up most of the night, deeply burdened to pray but not knowing exactly why. Next day, news began to reach Australia of an alleged communist coup in Indonesia which had been thwarted. Seven generals were dead. General Suharto, who was in charge of the President's bodyguard, had emerged as a new centre of power for the nation; he eclipsed and later replaced and arrested the previous President, Sukarno.

Suharto blamed the Indonesian Communist Party for planning the coup. Indonesia was suddenly convulsed with anti-communist violence and bloodshed. Thousands were murdered.

People began to ask Bruce and Annette if they shouldn't pray about going to some other country, or to a pastorate in Australia. One church made Bruce a very strong offer, 'We have prayed about it,' they told him, 'and we believe God would have you join us as our minister.' Even Bruce's WEC colleagues reminded him that there were many other needy areas where he and Annette could serve.

Bruce wouldn't hear any of it. God had promised him that he was going to Indonesia, and to Indonesia he would go. Somebody once introduced Bruce at a WEC meeting as 'This is Bruce Rattray, who hopes to go to Indonesia.'

'That's not right,' Bruce replied when he got to the microphone. 'This is Bruce Rattray who is going to Indonesia.'

Stewart Dinnen, who knew as much as anyone about what it is to take a stand of faith – believing in God's promises regardless of circumstances – stood solidly behind Bruce and Annette through the whole time. Others wondered if they were doing the right thing.

Almost a year passed before the situation in Indonesia made

another visa application possible. 1967 had dawned with no sign of progress. More months passed. WEC's patient business agent, Ramon Williams, made yet another speculative call on the immigration department in Jakarta to see what was happening with the Rattrays' latest visa application.

In protocol-heavy Indonesia, only the Departmental Head had authority to accept or decline visa applications. The woman in charge of Immigration who had repeatedly turned down the visa, reiterated that it was requested for an area of communist insurgency from Malaysia. No foreigners were welcome there.

Ramon assured her that they would be in Sintang, not the border area.

Then came the vocation aspect – what would they be doing in Kalimantan? Finally she admitted that the application would have a better chance if Bruce was coming to teach the local Indonesians about farming.

After a 'quick' (pre-internet) communication with Bruce and the supply of some certificates and diplomas, Ramon submitted the application with the assurance that Bruce wanted to come to 'help the locals improve their lifestyle'.

Her comment was, 'Why didn't you say that in the first place?' *VISA GRANTED.*

The lives of thousands of Dayaks would never be the same again.

TREKKING

16

As they travelled up the wide Kapuas River of West Kalimantan, Bruce and Annette were as excited as children. Along with two-year-old Paul, they had already spent six weeks in the provincial capital, Pontianak, and were now heading for Sintang. There, they were to spend the next eighteen months learning Indonesian.

Annette, weak and gaunt, was recuperating from a severe virus contracted in Pontianak. When, after prayer and medicine, Annette's condition had worsened, Bruce wept before the Lord. 'You called me so clearly all those years ago and worked miracles to get us here. Now we have only just arrived and it looks like I am going to lose Anne!'

At last he had prayed, 'Lord, I will never understand this, but I trust your loving sovereignty. Your will be done.' The next day, Dr Wendell Geary from the Conservative Baptist Hospital, over a day's travel away, unexpectedly arrived in Pontianak. It proved a turning point. They had no doubt he had been sent by God.

The mission boat they travelled on was an extraordinary craft built like a houseboat – long, narrow and top-heavy, its diesel engine thumping slowly through the mud-yellow water. The boat was steered by Fred (Woodi) Woodward, leader of the small WEC team. Woodi was based in Sintang, which was the main district administrative centre for the interior of West Kalimantan.

Woodi had spent years chugging up and down the rivers, and with his lawyer's eye for small print and precedent, had recorded every hidden rock and sandbar.

Dry season was the season for sandbars, however, and despite all his maps the boat beached itself several times. Freeing it could take hours of revving, rocking, and pushing with poles.

The scenery stayed much the same throughout the five-day journey – jungle-covered banks occasionally broken by a row of simple Malay houses and a *surau* (Muslim prayer house) or still more occasionally by a small town, with its Chinese bazaar and floating raft-houses bumping against the shoreline. Monkeys chattered in the trees and in the evenings, ravenous mosquitoes, whining like dentists' drills, feasted on them in the flame-light of fireflies.

Bruce and Annette's language-learning in Sintang proved to be much more 'learning' than language, the latter being acquired through books, intermittent teachers and mixing with the local Malays. But the endless variety of new experiences more than made up for that lack, the highlight being their trip up to the Iban area on the Sarawak border.

Bruce and Annette had the privilege of joining the little Iban fellowship, led by Pak Debu, for its first communion service. Pak Debu, whose dramatic conversion was known far and wide, was one of the first Iban converts on the Kalimantan side of the border. He was a fearless witness, and he and Bruce 'clicked' from the start, forming a bond that remained strong over the many years until his death.

It was April 1969 before Bruce and Annette finally started on what was to be their life's work. This time the houseboat pilot was Iain Mackenzie, a brisk and dry-witted Scottish WECer with a rather military bearing, who with his wife Margaret became great friends to the Rattrays. They didn't know it then, but the boat chugged past, in reverse order, the main places they would live for the next three decades.

First, half a day upriver from Sintang, they reached Nanga Lebang (Nanga means 'the mouth of the river'). This had been headquarters for the tiny team of WEC missionaries until Woodi had moved to Sintang. Now there was a clinic staffed by an Australian worker called Isabel Stephenson – the same lady whose challenging talk at Melbourne Bible Institute had so spoken to Annette. Isabel was to become a beloved colleague.

A few hours further upriver they came to the only traffic re-direction of the entire trip – leaving the Kapuas to its north-easterly direction, they turned north into the dark waters of the Ketungau River. After almost a day's travel up the winding Ketungau they arrived at Nanga Merakai. Here was the administrative centre for the Central Ketungau area where Bruce and Annette would spend perhaps the happiest decade of their lives.

They were now travelling north-westerly and finally, four hours further on, they came to the trading post (three Chinese families) of Nanga Sekalau. A few hundred metres further upriver was a wooden house where Isabel Stephenson and an

English WEC missionary, Gladys Rusha, had run a small clinic and a school. The house had been empty for a few years and the jungle had been working hard to take it back.

Iain and Bruce unloaded the Rattrays' few possessions and carried them up the slippery river bank: a kerosene-powered fridge; furniture, mostly handmade by Bruce; oil-drums containing clothing, books, household items and medical equipment. They cut the undergrowth back, arranged the furniture and hung a few pictures on the wall. Annette sewed curtains for the windows and drapes for doors in the grass-matting partitions.

Near to their home was a second house into which moved a young Dayak couple Adjuk and Esnad with their baby, Rus. Adjuk was from the Upper Ketungau (that is, the upper portion of the region through which the Ketungau River passes; most geography in Kalimantan is defined by the rivers).

He had been schooled for a time by Gladys Rusha and had just graduated from the Bible school run by the Christian and Missionary Alliance (CMA). CMA had been working in the interior for over thirty years, including the area west of the Ketungau River. The so-called 'WEC area' was the large region to the east of the river.

Iain and Margaret Mackenzie gave Bruce and Annette some orientation. Bruce was fidgety though. He didn't really want orientating. He just wanted Iain to leave, and for him and Adjuk to start trekking. Iain finally marched off into his boat for the two-day journey home (a day back down the Ketungau, a left turn onto the Kapuas, then a day back upriver again to the town of Semitau).

Thus, with Isabel a long day downriver at Nanga Lebang, and the Mackenzies two days away in Semitau, was the tiny WEC team spread. (The Woodward family were back in the US at this time, but their base was even further downriver in Sintang.)

Bruce and Annette, both loners, were happy. At last, at last, they could start their life's work. Paul, too, at three and a half, was in his element, taking to the jungle and the Dayaks with as much enthusiasm as his dad. His special project, though, was baby Rus!

17

We pause for a geography lesson: Bruce and Annette were living on the island of Borneo. The northern third of Borneo belonged to Malaysia and to the small Islamic Kingdom of Brunei. Malaysia's Borneo provinces were called Sabah and Sarawak. The rest of Borneo was Indonesian, and was called Kalimantan. The Ketungau Region, where Bruce and Annette were based, was a section of Western Kalimantan that bordered Sarawak.

The two families – one Western, one Dayak – were the only Christian workers for a wide area east/north-east of the Ketungau River up to the Sarawak border and across to the Iban areas. In April 1969 this was home to tens of thousands of Dayaks in several hundred long-house villages. This vast area was only navigable by river or by the jungle pathways, many of them called 'rat trails'.

Dayaks, one of the forgotten (and when remembered, despised) peoples of the earth, were slash-and-burn rice farmers, usually highly tattooed and ear-pierced. They also fished, and hunted with alarming home-made muzzle-loader guns. They would possibly have stayed off the map for decades more, had they not recently become one of the frontlines in the Cold War.

The national borders were meaningless to the jungle and the animals. Until recently, they had been meaningless to the Dayaks too. The mountainous border was mostly unmarked, so you could hike into Malaysia from Indonesia without knowing it.

The Confrontation with Malaysia (1964-66) had changed all this, making the invisible political lines a matter of life and death. Sarawak was home to ethnically-Chinese communist guerrillas and now, three years later, armed with watches, agricultural tools, cigarettes and clothing, they had infiltrated Kalimantan, trying to win the Dayaks over to their brand of communism.

Opposing them was the Indonesian army that had built bases at the bigger villages, and that ran patrols to find the guerrillas. The Government was building schools, trying to accelerate the 'development' of the Dayaks and make them more fully a part of Indonesia.

Caught in the middle were the Dayaks, with few ambitions beyond next year's harvest, and hardly even knowing they were Indonesians. To the Dayaks, exchanging rice for watches and radios with the guerrillas was a bargain in their favour, or so they thought, until they became the meat in the sandwich that both sides began to devour.

What might have been a lazy, half-hearted Cold War front had rather recently turned bloody and grim. Guerrilla units and army patrols ambushed each other. Each side had dragged Dayaks from their villages and shot them as informers.

Neither side cared much for the Dayaks, save in their role as pawns in the great game. Indonesian soldiers typically saw their fellow-countrymen as dirty, backward jungle-dwellers, a national embarrassment. On one occasion, they told Bruce that Dayaks 'had no souls; really, they were just like animals.' (You can imagine Bruce's response!)

Many times they would slap Dayaks in the face, or poke them with rifle butts, shaming and bullying them. A common technique was to soak them for hours in the cold waters of the small streams.

The CMA national church was established west of the Ketungau River but there was no organized Christianity to the east. The Roman Catholic priest from Sintang occasionally visited villages close to the river in the central Ketungau, and in the southern area a handful of villages professed Catholicism. Apart from WEC, no other Christian agency worked in the whole of the area east of the Ketungau River right across to the Kapuas and beyond. The Dayaks there were not a people with friends.

18

Bruce and Annette were easy targets for the communists. Just a few years earlier, half a dozen WEC workers had been killed by rebels in Central Africa. More recently still, one had been shot dead, and others had their house blown up around them by communist guerrillas in Vietnam.

Bruce didn't want to be any kind of a hero. But through prayer he came to a strong conviction that God was saying to him, *'I've placed you here for such a time as this. Now trek.'*

So he and Adjuk trekked. Adjuk had relatives in some of the villages they visited. He steered Bruce through the winding rat trails, up the rivers, and through the even more winding trails of Dayak culture. He translated from Bruce's simple Indonesian into the local dialect.

The two of them would set out from Nanga Sekalau by canoe and outboard motor. Or on more distant treks they would chug up the rivers in the small motorboat until there was no draught left, then moor the motorboat and climb into the canoe. When the water became too shallow for the canoe's large outboard motor, they would swap it for the small outboard, skimming between the floating logs, rocks, snapped-off tree branches and other debris.

Sometimes they would see a few hollowed-out log canoes moored by the river, a sign that a longhouse was a short distance away through the bush.

Or, when they finally ran out of water even for the canoe, they would put on their backpacks and hike through the green shade.

They began work in the Sekalau area of the Central Ketungau in June 1969, and it was not many months later that the turnings to the Christian faith began.

19

In those early days, the Dayaks were shy and suspicious as the strangers strode into their village. Bruce and Adjuk would be aware of women and children, who had almost no contact with the outside world, peeking with dark eyes through the cracks in the bark walls of the longhouse.

The two men would climb up the notched log onto the communal veranda and leave their packs outside the village head's doorway. Each door off the veranda was a family home. A larger village might have 20-30 doors, a family of perhaps ten people behind each door.

They would then bathe in the nearby river to freshen up. With evening approaching and the villagers returning from the rice-field, Bruce and Adjuk would ask permission to stay the night and speak.

Warm Dayak hospitality, and sometimes Adjuk's relatives, usually guaranteed a welcome. (That might not be the case if the village had been actively helping the communist guerrillas.)

A meal of rice and vegetables (maybe with a few tiny fish) would be cooked in the kitchen area out back by the headman's wife, then brought into the large family room to be served.

They'd all sit on a woven mat, with the dogs and pigs underneath fighting for any food that fell through the sapling floor.

After the meal was over, Bruce would speak, sitting on the veranda, the villagers packed closely around. He spoke by the fuzzy light of a kerosene lamp, the smoke from the mosquito fires below permeating the air and affecting more than the mosquitoes! He competed with buzzing insects, crying babies, growling dogs, snoring pigs and all the hoots and whines and rustles of the jungle night.

At first, Bruce used picture rolls to explain the gospel in Dayak terms – mainly The Two Ways (there was a graphic Dayak version) and The Bridge. Later he added Bible stories he had thoroughly prepared, and in those early days he used them again and again.

One of his favourites was the parable of the rich man and Lazarus in Luke 16, with its stark portrayal of life and death, heaven and hell, faith and unbelief.

'Now I am giving you the news about Jesus. He is the way to heaven. What are you going to do with what you have heard tonight?'

Another favourite was the parable of the prodigal son, adapted for the local scene. A brilliant storyteller, Bruce, eyes roving around his audience, would tell of the son wishing his father was dead, grabbing his inheritance, loading his father's wealth into a canoe, paddling all the way down to Sintang or even taking a boat to Pontianak, and squandering everything. And then returning in rags, so destitute that all he wanted was to be his father's *kuli* (labourer).

Once Bruce was describing the father pacing up and down

the veranda, longing to see his son again, when one old man suddenly jumped up in great excitement and exclaimed, 'You mean he still loved him? After all that, he still loved him?'

'Oh, yes. The father still loved him with all his heart.' (This never ceased to amaze them. In a society where unforgiveness, holding grudges and seeking revenge are the norm, this was beyond their understanding.)

Then Bruce would let them ask questions, and they would ask and talk, sometimes for hours, with Adjuk translating. And then they would discuss what to do. This puzzled Bruce at first, because his whole understanding of the Christian faith was that it was for an individual to decide, but the Dayaks always wanted to decide things together.

Sometimes they would say, 'we can't decide, we aren't all together,' or 'we'll decide when the village head gets back.'

'Never mind about waiting for the village head,' Bruce used to say, until he knew better, 'it's your soul. You decide. You are responsible.'

Indonesia has five officially-recognized faiths: Islam, Buddhism, Hinduism, and the Protestant and Catholic varieties of Christianity. The Dayaks were coming under enormous pressure from the Indonesian Army to adopt one of these. It was seen as part of their development as Indonesian citizens, and as a bulwark against communism.

So sometimes they would talk far into the night, and at some point (Bruce could never pinpoint quite when, though everyone else could) it would become clear that the whole village, or sometimes just several households, were ready to *masuk jalan Tuhan* ('enter the Lord's way').

20

Bruce lived to trek in those early years. When he got up in the morning, it was the first thing on his mind. When he extinguished the kerosene lamp at night, his head was still buzzing with plans and prayers.

With Adjuk's help, he drew a picture-map of the entire Ketungau Region, marking each village. He figured he was likely to be here for three years before returning to Australia for home leave, and he resolved to preach the gospel in every one of these hundreds of villages in those three years.

He wrote long letters back to his dad describing each village in detail, the names of the leaders, the particular characteristics, the problems, trying to give his dad raw materials that he could turn into prayer. Warren had organized a prayer group at home and with all of his extraordinary energy was wrestling in prayer for his son.

Bruce had a compelling sense that now was the time for the Ketungau Dayaks. He trekked and trekked. It would not be unusual to be away for ten days, spend a few nights at home with Annette and Paul, then set off again in the morning for another ten days. He always prayed for guidance about which village he should visit, and was gratified to find a village that he had sensed a distinctive leading to visit, turning wholesale to the Christian faith.

Nothing was going to deflect him from God's call, as was shown in an incident that was highly significant, because it involved the first major response.

Adjuk's baby Rus came down with a high fever the night before Bruce and Adjuk were due to leave. This could be serious – malaria or other tropical fevers are often fatal for small children.

Bruce and Annette saw this as a satanic hindrance, so prayed against it. The fatalism of animism permeates every area of a Dayak's life and this worldview is not readily thrown off when one becomes a Christian. Adjuk was fearful, so would not go. But Bruce needed him.

'Annette can look after Rus,' Bruce insisted. 'We've prayed for this village for so long and we must go.' Eventually, after more prayer, Adjuk reluctantly agreed. Annette spent a watchful night with Rus, whose fever settled the next day.

It turned out to be a God-ordained trip. Bruce showed his picture roll at the village where the village head was named Juanggak. He was also the *Ketua Adat* (cultural head) for the whole of the Sekalau River area.

That night he decided to enter the Lord's Way, with almost the whole village joining him.

It so happened that the head of another large village was also there. He had had a dream the previous night and was amazed to see similarities between the dream and the picture roll. He asked Bruce to come home with him and show it to his people, so the next night almost the whole of his village entered *Jalan Tuhan* as well. (Although these men may never have come to personal faith in Christ and their villages showed few signs of spiritual life until years later, God used that visit to open the door to the gospel into the whole of the Sekalau River area.)

Another time in those early days, Paul, after waving his dad off on yet another trek, said to Annette, 'I think Daddy loves the Dayaks more than he loves us.'

That made Bruce think deeply, but as he weighed it up in his mind, he decided that the Dayaks had no-one. Christ's command and God's obvious timing meant that Bruce needed to be obedient and bring the gospel to them. Now was the time for the Dayaks; travel was slow and difficult; necessarily Bruce had to be away from home for a large part of the time.

For Bruce and Annette it was a believing obedience – an obedience that took literally Jesus' words in Matthew 6:33. If they *'sought first the Kingdom of God'* they could also trust the same Jesus to provide everything Paul (and later their second child Simon) needed. It was a decision that they still didn't regret half a lifetime later, seeing how everything turned out.

21

Annette's ministry in those early months was as extraordinary (and actually as brave) as Bruce's. She ran a clinic and dispensary. She was also bringing up a small child in a very remote and dangerous area – no modern amenities, no doctors, phones or shops. The only fresh food was whatever they could catch in the river, pluck from the forest or buy from visiting patients.

Paul thrived. With the jungle at his door, the animals and birds were a constant source of interest, including the abundant snakes, scorpions and centipedes. Paul never needed entertaining, as during the hours Annette spent treating the sick, he would join her, obviously enjoying his front seat view. Tiring of that, he would visit Rus, who now had a baby sister, or 'make something' with his tools. Fortunately he was not yet old enough to want to hunt or paddle a canoe. That came later!

During the short dry season, a white sandbank would appear across the river. Annette remembers many happy evenings, paddling to this private beach, bathing, teaching Paul to swim, catching a fish for supper, then paddling home before night fell. Even the possibility of snakes (they swim very well) or a rare crocodile did not dampen their enjoyment. Of course, if Dad was home too, it was lots more fun.

Returning from one of his early trips, Bruce produced from his jacket a scrawny little brown puppy. Scamp became Paul's inseparable companion and faithful watchdog, until his death from a *belantik* (a bamboo spear sprung as a trap for wild pigs) while they were on leave.

It was a rare day that Annette didn't see a few canoes sliding down the black waters of the Ketungau River carrying people for her to treat. Alongside the two mission houses was another flimsy bark structure they called 'The Hospital', used as an overnight facility and for patients needing longer-term care.

Her ministry dovetailed beautifully with Bruce's. Her clinic was much more about Christian love than Western wonder-drugs. Bruce and Annette bought the medicines themselves, which were nearly all Indonesian-made. The difference was in how they were applied – with skill, love and faith.

People often wouldn't come to the clinic until they were in

their last extremity of need. A deaf and dumb man presented himself, for example, with a huge ulcer on his upper arm. It had eaten right into his armpit and down to the bone. The government clinic had told him to go to the hospital in Sintang to have the arm amputated.

Annette was involved for weeks carefully irrigating and dressing the wound twice daily. Eventually it was completely healed. 'I did not regret one minute of the hours I spent cleaning that revolting ulcer,' Annette said later. It was the combination of cheap drugs on unsuspecting jungle bacteria, good medical practice, lots of prayer, and Christian love that made Annette's treatments so effective.

22

A wide open door for ministry had opened to Bruce and Annette, and they were drawing on all the lessons learnt in the years of waiting.

Rainfall was around 100 inches a year, an inch every three or four days, except in the dry season. It peaked when tropical monsoon clouds shook themselves out on the highlands, sluicing unthinkable masses of water throughout Kalimantan. The rivers could rise or fall metres in a single day, flooding large areas. This had spectacular consequences for the mosquitoes, other parasites, and water-borne bacteria.

In the middle of Bruce and Annette's first wet season at Nanga Sekalau, news reached Annette of an epidemic of vomiting and diarrhoea, sweeping away many children, typically those under three years old. From one village alone, 16 children arrived in a fleet of canoes at Annette's clinic.

Annette put them in 'The Hospital' and started teaching their parents oral rehydration therapy. She gave each parent a big bottle of water with added salt and sugar, instructing them to spoon-feed the children. She insisted that they not be given solid food (rice) until she said so.

Three children quickly recovered and went home but Annette soon realized that the remaining children weren't getting any better. Some were worse. To her horror, she discovered that their parents were still feeding them rice and throwing the water out!

Adjuk's wife Esnad then explained to Annette that rice was given even to someone about to die, such was the importance of its 'life-giving' properties. They had to have rice, and the spirit-healers taught that the only way to treat diarrhoea was not to give water. This was a strong and binding *pantang* (taboo) and the parents were terrified of breaking it. Even when their children cried out for water, they refused them – and so they died.

When she learnt this, something like holy indignation began to smoulder in Annette. She took herself to her room and went to prayer. Like Bruce, she skipped naturally between theology and life. If she was united with Christ, she was also, as the Bible describes, seated with Christ in heavenly places, and in a position of authority far above all the power of the spirit-world with its spells and prohibitions.

On her knees before God, she began to rebuke the enemy who was holding these people captive. John 10:10 was the verse she used. (*'The thief comes only to steal and kill and destroy; I have come that they may have life, and have it to the full.'*) The devil had stolen, killed and destroyed the souls of the Dayaks for centuries, taboos like this being one of the tools. Jesus had come to destroy his power and bring abundant life. She told the spirits directly that the power of the gospel had come now and it was time to overthrow their lies with truth.

She returned to the hospital and patiently explained that this *pantang* was causing their children to die whereas Jesus had come to give life. She insisted that if they did not follow her instructions they would have to go home.

They probably understood very little of what she said, but this time the parents listened and the fact that they all stayed meant God had won a victory and lives were saved. She continued to treat them until they were all improved enough to go home. Only one child did not recover because his mother had clung to the *pantang*. After arriving home she fed him rice. The next morning he was dead. This news spread throughout the area. 'They still did not understand or believe,' Annette said later. 'But the enemy lost a lot of ground.'

Further afield the *pantang* continued to take lives. Fifteen years later at Nanga Lebang, Annette treated a child almost too dehydrated to save. With tears streaming down his face the boy's father cried, 'If only I had known! I have lost four children because of the *pantang*.' This was not uncommon.

23

A few months into their ministry, the conviction came over Bruce that it was time to visit some of the villages in the Upper Sekalau region, further up the Sekalau River towards Sarawak. This was the worst and deadliest area for guerrilla activity. He had already been given reluctant permission by the army commander of the area, stressing that they could not take any responsibility for his safety. Bruce assured them that he was in God's hands. He decided to walk in – a very long trek. By not using the noisy outboard motor, he hoped that he and Adjuk would not attract the attention of the guerrillas.

Just as they were arriving at their chosen village for the night, they heard the one cry guaranteed to make anyone's hair stand on end – the horrible, anguished death wail. They learnt that the communists had shot the village head as an informer. He had been rushed to hospital in Sintang. The news of his death had arrived at the village about the same time as Bruce and Adjuk.

The next day, the people told Bruce that it would be even more dangerous if they travelled further north and east. Bruce, however, had read a verse in his Bible that morning. It said, *'Do not be afraid; keep on speaking, do not be silent. For I am with you, and no-one is going to attack and harm you, because I have many people in this city'* (Acts 18:9-10).

Next, some children came running back to the longhouse. They'd seen men with guns while they were walking to the school in the next village. Bruce weighed things up again and still decided to go on, on the basis of the Bible verse. He left

Adjuk at the first village, to preach the gospel there, while he went on alone.

Half an hour into his journey, he turned a corner in the rat trail and found himself facing three ragged men pointing machine guns at him.

'Who are you?' they asked quickly. 'What are you doing here? Where have you come from?'

Bruce looked at them, feeling his heart enveloped in a great peace. He quickly offered up a silent prayer for Annette and Paul.

'I'm a *pendeta* (minister of religion). I live in Nanga Sekalau and I'm going to the village of Lubuk Kedang to bring them the gospel.'

They talked among themselves, and slowly lowered their guns. Bruce realized with enormous relief that despite their rags they were soldiers, not guerrillas.

They escorted him to the army post at Lubuk Kedang, and introduced him to the lieutenant in charge, who told him that he was pleased that Bruce was here, because the Dayaks needed a religion. Bruce told them that he wanted to hold a gospel meeting, but before he did he would like to walk a couple of hours more through the jungle to still one more village, so that he could invite them also.

'There's a fair degree of danger in that,' the lieutenant told him. Bruce, remembering the way God had spoken that morning, told the soldier, 'the Lord will look after me.'

So he set off again. This time, marching down the rat trail, he suddenly felt the hairs rising on the back of his neck, as if he were being watched. Heart beating fast, he carried on – nothing else to do – every sense straining, expecting any minute to hear a rifle-bolt click. Nothing happened.

He arrived at the village, invited them, and set off back to Lubuk Kedang, where he held a fairly large meeting with some good responses. The next day, he picked up Adjuk and they eventually made their way home.

Years later he learnt that five Chinese guerrillas confessed that they had had him in their sights while he walked that day. Three had wanted to kill him, two had disagreed, and while they were arguing among themselves, Bruce had marched right out of view.

For some time following this incident, whenever Bruce was leaving for a trip, the last thing he'd hear as he pulled away from the bank was Paul calling out, 'Goodbye Dad. Don't get shot, will you?' Once Bruce's boat was out of sight, though, Paul would climb up the bank, happily chattering to Annette.

24

Bruce was having the time of his life: trekking through the jungle day after day, or storming up the rivers in his boat; preaching the gospel, and seeing people turn to the Christian faith, village after village.

Bruce knew that the Dayaks were turning to Christianity with little understanding, for mixed motives, under Army pressure. Surely it wasn't genuine. WEC workers had seen a village-wide turning to Christianity once before in the early

1960s, in the far south of the WEC area. It hadn't been encouraging. Few people seemed to have truly broken with the old ways. The early team believed that individual conversion was best.

Yet for all his doubts, Bruce had such a burning from God in his heart that he knew he mustn't stop trekking and preaching. Woe to him if he stopped!

The foolishness of what he was doing was obvious on every hand. For example, when a village turned to the *Jalan Tuhan* Bruce had to register them with the department of religion. This collision of third-world bureaucracy and tattooed tribesmen was enormous fun for all concerned, except perhaps the bureaucrats trying to make sense of the forms.

'So now tell me how old you are,' Bruce would ask a Dayak man.

'Ah.' Many smiles, much thinking. 'I think I'm about 32.'

'OK. 32. And how old is your oldest son?'

'My oldest son? Hmm.' More thinking. 'He's about 28.'

'I see. So you are 32 … and your son is 28 … ?'

The reports that worried Bruce more were those that went home, and came back in magazines saying, 'Massive turning to Christ in West Kalimantan.'

Bruce knew very well that he was not seeing a massive turning to Christ. He was seeing the Dayaks turn en masse to the Christian faith, which gave them a huge opportunity genuinely to turn to Christ.

A group movement was one thing, personal transformation another. He was always careful in his letters home to talk about a 'turning to the Christian faith' rather than a turning to Christ, but he was usually misunderstood.

Helped by correspondence with his old friend Stewart Dinnen, Bruce began a crash course in group movements to the Christian faith. He subscribed to a newsletter that analysed similar movements around the world and through history. He learnt that, far from being exceptional, group movements to the Christian faith, followed up by patient teaching and discipleship, were the normal way that the Christian faith spread through the world.

Europe, for example, was evangelized tribe by tribe. A local chief might lead his people to adopt the Christian faith. The tribe would become Christians, throw out the old gods, turn their temples into churches, and revise their customs. After that, they might see the ebb and flow of spiritual life within that overall framework – revivals and fallings away; but the tribe remained 'Christian'.

Bruce saw that the 'people movement' among the Dayaks of the Ketungau was a tangled thing. It was a collective act of great significance because they were letting down the drawbridge to the fortress of their animistic culture. But it was only a beginning.

For centuries, the Dayaks had believed lies: they had masses of rules and superstitions intended to protect them from the spirits. Those rules had to be replaced with the truth.

But where to get the new teaching they needed? Most Dayaks spoke only little Indonesian; only some of the younger ones could read. Some villages had only been visited once or twice, others only once in many months. The miracle was that any did take the gospel to heart.

Take Parnu, for example, a young man who lived about a two-hour canoe trip from Bruce and Annette's home. After he became a Christian, he explained to them,

'I am no longer afraid to go to the rice field or hunting on my own. I know Jesus is with me.' This loss of fear was a clear evidence of genuine faith in Christ.

He came from a family of powerful witchdoctors and needed further prayer to be delivered from all the occult involvement and influence. But this gentle, sensitive man did change and became the spiritual leader in his village – an example of how some did, even in the earliest days, really grasp the gospel and were in turn grasped by it.

25

Dayaks instinctively wanted new rules – a new tribal code. All their life had been rules. Bruce knew that teaching new rules would be a fatal error. The Christian faith is grace and love, not rules. So he tried to get them to think out their own responses:

'If we become Christians, do we have to give up drinking?'

'Well, do you think that the drunken feasts please God?'

'I suppose not.' Dayaks were no different from the rest of the planet when it came to drunken parties.

It was only drinking (along with gambling and hunting) that shook them out of their habitual lethargy – a lethargy caused by fatalism, a very low protein diet, malaria and the enervating climate.

They would continue: 'Would it be all right to drink just a little bit, so long as you keep yourself under control?'

'What do you think?'

'Well, I think – yes. But then I think, how many of us can drink just a little bit?'

The drinking at a *gawai* (feast) was so spectacular that not only the men and women got drunk: so did the children, and even the dogs and pigs. And drinking *bram* (rice wine), with its unknown alcoholic content, could have devastating results.

Some of the new Christians knew other Dayaks from further west who had turned to the Christian faith under the ministry of the CMA. They had rules (despite the efforts of the early missionaries) which they were happy to pass on. One way or another, the freedom of a life lived under the grace of God was not being grasped by too many.

On top of all the problems of learning new ways, the old Dayak order of life was itself in danger of passing away, squeezed to death in the scrum between the superpowers. They told Bruce, 'It's like our old longhouse has burnt down and we haven't yet built a new one.'

Many forest peoples, similarly rammed by modernity, have simply died out. It was because of the Dayaks' resilience and much prayer that this did not happen.

At the same time, Bruce's sketch map of the Ketungau Region stood in his prayer hut as a permanent reminder that he was going to reach every single village with the gospel.

This was his priority. God had commanded him to preach the gospel to them all, and he was going to do it in his first three years.

Bruce and Annette prayed for each other, their sons, the new believers, their co-workers; they cried out to God for extra people to come and help with the heavy load.

They wrote letters to share their prayer burden with the scores of prayer partners at home, especially with their fathers (not all reached their destination). Annette's father, Allen Tidey, lovingly known as 'Gramps', was, like Warren Rattray, a man of prayer. Much that was done for the Kingdom of God among the Dayaks was the result of the prayers of these faithful prayer partners.

26

Two-way radios helped the widely-scattered team keep in contact. A call from Iain Mackenzie brought a happy surprise and a remarkable answer to prayer. Iain was down in Sintang on business and met four young evangelists who had been sent via the WEC-related Bible School in Java on a year's placement to Kalimantan. Bruce and Annette rushed down (as fast as you can in a motorboat on a slow-flowing river to a town that is over a day's travel away).

These men had come from the Indonesian province of West Timor, which was enjoying a revival of the Christian faith, and they were raring to go! Bruce and Annette brought them back to Nanga Sekalau and had them out in two villages within a week.

These young Timorese came at just the right time and their qualities of enthusiasm, faith and perseverance delighted Bruce and Annette. They were utterly passionate in prayer, preaching and service for the Dayaks, despite suffering enormous culture shock and loneliness.

Their contribution is not really recorded anywhere else, but Bruce and Annette counted them and their successors as vital co-workers. Three of them became like sons. Napthali, one of the original four, and Alfonsus, who came later, are still serving the Lord in West Kalimantan as this book is being written.

27

The small town of Nanga Merakai was about four hours downriver from Bruce and Annette's base at Nanga Sekalau. Increasingly they were drawn there. It had the only junior secondary school in the whole of the Ketungau, a police and army post, a district government office and a few shops.

Bruce had been asked to preach in the small church and to teach religious education in the high school. Seeing this as a strategic way of reaching a new generation of Dayaks, he began spending every other weekend in the town.

The leader of the Protestant congregation in Merakai was also deputy district superintendent. Pak Migi had more than once urged Bruce to move his whole base down to Nanga Merakai. It was strategic for the whole region, much more than their current base at Nanga Sekalau.

Bruce was not quick to receive advice from others, lest he was deflected from what he knew God had clearly shown him. He didn't want the distractions of moving house. Yet he and

Annette had moved to Nanga Sekalau originally only because of the mission house already there, and they had been feeling a little uneasy about whether it was the best long-term place for their work.

Bruce (as the Ketungau region's only resident *pendeta*, or minister of religion) often attended regional strategy meetings hosted by the local military and government officials. He made many good contacts at these meetings and often found the path smoothed by the Indonesian authorities for his evangelism. These meetings confirmed that Nanga Merakai was to be the new regional centre. Still though, Bruce lingered, not having heard personally and clearly from God.

One day in late 1970, eighteen months after they had arrived in the Ketungau, Bruce was steering the in-board diesel boat (the *Utusan Injil* or 'Gospel Messenger') up the Ketungau River. The boat was crowded with people who had suddenly 'discovered' they had vital business upstream and had flagged him down for a free river-taxi ride.

They had just left the little township of Nanga Merakai behind and the *Utusan Injil* was thumping up the black river at its steady eight knots. As the boat rounded the bend opposite the mouth of the Merakai River, it passed the large house built by a Chinese trader named Pak Acap, who owned an enormous rubber plantation. It was one of the few proper houses in the Ketungau, made of wooden boards rather than the customary bark walls and sapling floors.

Because of the insurgency, all the Chinese traders in the upper and central Ketungau were being ordered to pack up and leave, even though some had lived there for generations. They were forbidden to sell houses, rubber plantations or pepper gardens. The army confiscated everything!

Pak Acap, having been forewarned, had quickly moved his family and his possessions to Sintang and began trying to sell his house and rubber plantations. Pak Migi heard about this and urged Bruce to buy the house himself.

As they chugged past in the *Utusan Injil*, Bruce felt an immediate urge that he should indeed buy the house. Normally, he liked to pray and wait on God to be sure about big decisions. This time, the impression was so strong and the sense of urgency so great that he set about it straight away.

The next morning, he took Annette and Paul in the houseboat back down the river to Nanga Merakai. He talked with the church leader. He also found out more about the house. Motoring back upriver again, they moored the houseboat and went into the deserted property for a closer look. It was a large, well-made wooden house with acres of rubber trees surrounding it – plenty of space for now and more to develop.

They felt completely confirmed that this was God's place for them. Hand in hand (Bruce enjoyed this kind of faith-act enormously) they walked round the property seven times, praying and claiming it for God's kingdom.

Back home again at Nanga Sekalau, Bruce radioed Woodi and told him he wanted to buy this property and that he was coming down river again to talk about it.

Woodi was a famously cautious decision-maker. And the decision involved mission finance. Bruce spent just about the whole day's trip downriver in prayer, as did Annette, in between supervising Paul and providing endless cups of coffee for the *penumpang* (passengers).

Woodi was instantly enthusiastic, which Bruce saw as a minor miracle. Woodi also told him that he had a friend in the land office in Sintang. Early the next day Bruce and Woodi were on their way together further downriver.

Amazingly, it took them just a single day to agree the sale and sign all the papers. In the bureaucratic jungle that is Indonesia this was more unlikely an outcome than Woodi making a spur-of-the-moment decision. But it happened.

Returning late the next day to Nanga Sekalau, Bruce and Annette moored the *Utusan Injil* outside their new home.

Early in the morning a runner came with a letter. It was from the local Army commander who wanted to see Bruce immediately. Bruce went, and after the preliminaries were over, the commander explained to him carefully that he hoped Bruce wasn't thinking of trying to buy Pak Acap's house. This was an army area, no transactions were possible, and so it would be out of the question.

Stripped of Indonesian cultural attachments (which made the actual meeting far longer), the conversation then proceeded like this:

'As it happens,' Bruce said quietly, 'We have already bought it.'

'But you can't!'

'Well we did.'

'It's impossible!'

'Here are the papers.'

'I don't believe it!'

'Well, look at the papers.'

'Hmph!'

'As you can see, they are all in order.'

'In that case I suppose I'll just have to let you have it.'

So in late 1970 Bruce and Annette moved down to Nanga Merakai, to the home that their hearts, in some ways, were never subsequently to leave. Paul was five years old, and Annette, having had a miscarriage while living in Sintang, was pregnant again.

They didn't know, but after the miracle of the property, a deep trial was awaiting them.

28

Adjuk and Esnad were still at Sekalau, but the plan was for them to relocate to the far north of the Ketungau Region along with Yoktan, one of the Timorese evangelists. There they could evangelise that enormous area and strengthen the few little Christian groups.

The two moves – one to the strategic centre of Nanga Merakai in the Central Ketungau, one to the Upper Ketungau – together made a major step forward for developing the work in the whole of the Ketungau Region. This move didn't go uncontested, however.

Bruce and Annette were accompanied to Merakai by their teenage helper, a Dayak girl named Giah. She was a second-generation Christian from the CMA-founded church: as Bruce and Annette were to find out, that often meant you had a mental acceptance of the Gospel but not a personal experience of Christ.

Within a week of their arrival at Nanga Merakai, Giah began acting strangely. She kept saying to Annette, 'People paddling past our house are shouting insults at me.' This was baffling. Annette didn't hear anything. And people there didn't do that kind of thing.

Most of the time Giah was her normal self, helping Annette – who was five months pregnant now – settle in, look after Paul and set up the new clinic. Soon afterwards, Giah returned to her home village for a break.

A week later Bruce and Annette received an alarming letter. Giah was ill. She would wake up in the night, screaming uncontrollably, wild-eyed, thrashing around with superhuman strength and foaming at the mouth. It took four adults to hold her down.

Was it cerebral malaria? Or was she, as the Dayaks thought, demonized? The family wanted Bruce to come and take her back to Nanga Merakai.

Bruce trekked over to the village and stayed the night, ready to take Giah back the next morning. At 2:30 am precisely, with the longhouse as quiet as it ever got, Giah suddenly began to scream. By the time Bruce reached her, she was wild-eyed, foaming at the mouth, four men restraining her.

Bruce commanded the spirits, in the name of the Lord Jesus, to stop troubling her, and the manifestations stopped. The next morning Bruce set off, accompanied by several members of her family. Giah was being carried in a basket chair on a man's back.

Bruce was deeply worried about Giah and as they strode along, he started praying for her under his breath. Immediately, Giah cried out, 'Get him away from me! Get him away from me!' She could not have heard him. Previously Giah had treated Bruce like a father but now, eyes blazing with hatred, she could not bear to see him.

They arrived back at Nanga Merakai. That night, at 2:30am exactly, Giah again started screaming and thrashing around and only settled when Bruce commanded the spirits to be quiet.

It was a difficult time. They were preparing for the long trip to the Upper Ketungau to move Yoktan and Adjuk and family. Giah would suddenly flip into terrifying manifestations, and Bruce and Annette were spending weary hours in prayer, seeking the source of the problem, which they were sure was demonic. And although she tried, Giah couldn't talk.

Bruce deeply disliked this kind of ministry, even though he had seen dramatic and liberating results. After a day of prayer and fasting for Giah, Bruce commanded a dumb spirit to leave her, and she began to talk.

Giah's mother and two other family members were staying with her in the same room (as was quite normal). Giah told Bruce that her mother had spirit-fetishes and her cousin was a liar and a thief. This explained why they had not been able to achieve much. Bruce suggested these family members either repent or go home. They chose to go home and with them went much of the heaviness and opposition.

After further prayer and fasting, they felt that several strong demons still controlled Giah. When Bruce commanded them to leave, strange voices came from Giah's chest – in Indonesian, in the local dialect, and in what sounded like Arabic, arguing about who would leave. Bruce quoted scriptures that spoke of Christ's victory over the devil and insisted they all go. And they did.

Giah was like a limp rag doll afterwards but at last she was able to eat, sleep and talk normally.

Bruce would still not leave Giah alone with Annette, so he had asked one of the elders to preach that Sunday. Giah was standing by the front door when she began to tremble.

She had seen the Malay *dukun* from downriver coming around the side of the house. (A *dukun* is a spirit-practitioner who is able, for a fee, to perform spells and curses and attempt healings.) Annette saw him too and called out, asking if he were sick. (She knew he wasn't as this was Sunday when normally they would be at church!) The *dukun* mumbled something and left with a scowl.

Bruce, meanwhile, thought he had heard some rustling underneath the house. He went down to take a look and found a small bundle, tied up with dry grass, which he promptly burnt.

Not long after this, the students from the high school were preparing to go home for the holidays. Giah expressed a wish to join them. Giah's church had sent a letter saying that she should stay with the Rattrays until she was fully recovered. Bruce and Annette also insisted that she stay.

But Giah was determined to go and secretly made plans to leave – and she began to deteriorate. Soon, she was having episodes of pure madness – burning her own hands over the wood fire, slashing Scamp with a machete. 'A time,' Annette recalled, 'I would gladly forget.'

They continued with prayer sessions, but felt they'd hit a roadblock. It was as if Giah's quiet rebellion had opened the door once more to the spirits that had left. During one session they asked Giah who was troubling her. She turned her wild black eyes on them and spat, 'Satan! Satan! Satan!'

'Remarkably,' Annette recalled, 'through the weeks of this extremely stressful situation, we were very conscious of God's hand upon us, especially upon Paul. He was our deepest concern as we had no opportunity to send him away or contact home to ask for prayer cover. Yet he had no ill effects and happily 'paddled his own canoe' (literally), played with the dog or made sandcastles, hardly aware of the drama being played out. Only the God of the universe could do that!'

The day arrived for the move to the Upper Ketungau. Bruce was determined that this long-planned forward move wasn't going to be thwarted. They all piled into the motorboat, including Giah, who could not be left, and set off on the two-day trip upriver.

Giah had episodes of being highly disturbed, and again Bruce and the others would calm her down through prayer. Then, on the second day, unexpectedly, she leapt up, ran into the toilet cubicle at the stern, and bolted the door. Here you could reach down to scoop up river water to bathe. Or you could jump into the river! Giah refused to come out, so Bruce was forced to smash the door open with his shoulder. There was Giah sitting on the edge, swaying, trying to decide whether to throw herself in.

Annette began to have mild contractions. She was a nurse and midwife, and was not easily flustered. These could be false contractions. She told Bruce that she would rest until they settled.

With Adjuk making sure Giah didn't get away again, Giah sat and fixed her wild eyes on Annette, who was lying on one of the bunks, and stared and stared.

The contraction became stronger but more difficult was the oppressive sense of evil that she was feeling as Giah stared at her. It was almost like a physical pressure on her body.

'Bruce,' she said, 'you've got to get her away from me! These contractions are getting worse!'

On such a small boat, 'away' was not very far, so there was nothing to do but to keep motoring up the river, the whole party silently praying. With much relief, they were able to hand Giah over to some distant cousins at the village, which was right by the river bank. The rest of the party slept in the village, while Bruce, Annette and Paul spent the night in the houseboat.

It was a hard and restless night, with the contractions still coming. But it was also, like many a dark night, not without the presence of God.

Annette remembered: 'We knew that the enemy was at work through Giah and we weren't lying down to that. Bruce had dealt with Satan in authoritative prayer and we were maintaining our stand against him. And underneath was that quiet knowing the loving sovereignty of God that gives a confidence that nothing can move – even the uncertainty and natural fear of not knowing what was going to happen.'

Morning came. It was Sunday, and Bruce was to preach at the service. Before he set off, Bruce and Annette spent a little time together in worship and prayer. Annette's contractions continued but the deep oppression had lifted with the departure of Giah.

Bruce felt they should sing a hymn together, and he picked one of their favourites:

In heavenly love abiding,
No change my heart shall fear;
... The storm may roar without me,
My heart may low be laid;
But God is round about me,
And can I be dismayed?

By the end of the second verse they were both crying.

... He knows the way he taketh;
And I will walk with him.

They finally managed all the way through the hymn and Bruce prayed, quietly handing the unborn child and themselves over to Jesus – leaving it all with him, a deep and strange experience; in a way, their own Gethsemane.

Bruce climbed up the bank and walked a dozen paces over to the church. 'What shall I preach about?' he thought. An extremely odd Bible verse immediately came into his mind: *'When they began to sing and to praise, the Lord sent ambushes against the enemy'* (2 Chronicles 20:22, KJV).

So he preached on it, wondering what on earth the listeners would make of it, and deep down knowing he was preaching for himself. After the service was over, he rushed back to Annette in the boat.

'How are you?'

'Oh, about the same. What did you preach on?'

'If I let you have a hundred guesses you would never guess what I preached on.'

'Give me one guess. You preached on 2 Chronicles 20:22.'

'Someone came down and told you!'

'Nobody came. The moment you walked up the bank the

Lord brought that verse to my mind and I've been lying here praising the Lord and meditating on it ever since.'

Bruce and Annette asked for the child's life back again, and they both knew that it was going to be all right. Slowly, the contractions ebbed away.

They successfully installed Yoktan, Adjuk and family in the Upper Ketungau and returned home.

It was Christmas and they were to have spent it up in the Sekalau area. Because Annette was still on bed rest, Bruce set off alone, but to her surprise, he arrived back home the next night, having spent Christmas Day at Parnu's village two hours upriver. He had been stopped from entering the Sekalau because of a shootout and killing of some guerrillas about a kilometre behind their old Sekalau house!

Six weeks later, they received a letter from Bruce's dad. After his usual greetings he asked, 'Whatever were you doing on these two nights?' – and he cited the two dates when Giah had woken with demonic manifestations. 'I was woken up in the early hours with a vision of you, blood pouring down your face, as if you'd been scratched by a wild animal.'

Three months later, Bruce and Annette's second son, Simon, was born safely at the Conservative Baptist hospital on the west coast.

Sadly, however, Giah returned to her village, where her family immediately took her to witchdoctors. This was one of the most painful things for Bruce and Annette in the whole episode. Here were 'Christians' with the same attitude as the heathen: *asal sembuh* ('as long as he/she gets better'). They were blinded by the lie that they could tap into the devil's power as well as God's. So whoever did it – *'asal sembuh'*!

Giah became violent and dangerous so, as was customary in their culture, they built a small cage for her. She had periods of normality when she was able to work, but, tragically, the last years of her life were spent in the cage.

29

Nothing gave Bruce and Annette more joy than seeing lives transformed by the gospel.

They had come to know an educated Dayak named Yefta, who was head teacher of the primary school at Nanga Merakai.

Yefta had been brought up in one of the 'Christian' villages west of the Ketungau River.

A good-looking man with a warm smile, he was the treasurer of the Protestant group at Nanga Merakai, which was really the only organized Christian church in the whole WEC area. All the other congregations were village meetings on long-house verandas, most of them irregular, especially if they didn't have a leader.

Yefta had married one of his pupils. His schoolgirl wife had produced four children. Two had died before Bruce and Annette knew the family, and a third, a boy the same age as Paul, suddenly died from a fever while Bruce and Annette were away downriver, leaving Yefta and his wife with just one baby daughter.

On their arrival back, Bruce and Annette received the sad news of the death and that Yefta had taken his little family back to his village. Yefta's father was a *dukun*. With solemn blood-sacrifices Yefta had dedicated himself, his family and his posterity to Satan.

This was not unusual, even for 'Christians'; it was almost the Dayak equivalent of taking out life insurance. You gave yourself to Satan and he looked after you. (Even if Dayaks had never heard Christ's name, they all knew Satan's.)

Bruce and Annette noticed that Yefta's face had become somehow darkened and his demeanour heavy. They also knew that his life made a mockery of his so-called Christian profession, and they were praying for his salvation.

As the months passed, their prayer-burden for Yefta seemed to lighten. Bruce actually told Annette that he didn't think it would be long before God would 'draw Yefta in'.

One day, Yefta paddled up to their house in his canoe. As Bruce saw him coming up the bank, he called to Annette, 'Put on the coffee! Yefta has come to repent!'

After the required preliminaries (at least 10 minutes of social talk), Yefta started pouring out the long story of all he had done wrong, desperate to get out from under the burden of guilt that had begun to crush him.

Bruce kept explaining the gospel to him – 'No matter what you've done or for how long or to whom, Jesus has paid your debts and will forgive them all if you repent and turn to him.'

Still Yefta went on. 'But I've been using the church money for gambling!' He was utterly miserable, deeply under conviction of his sin, terrified of God's anger and the certainty of hell. He had already secretly paid the money back but it had not lightened the burden of guilt.

When he had finally finished, Bruce gently encouraged him to turn away from it all and ask Jesus to forgive him. Yefta did. The heavy burden seemed to fall away from him and he was overflowing with a sense of joy and forgiveness.

Later on, Bruce was able to visit the family and help them renounce all their pledges to Satan and commit themselves to Jesus as Lord.

A little later still, Annette led Yefta's wife to a clear personal faith for herself. Not too long after that, she fell pregnant again. Their tragic family situation was being reclaimed and healed.

30

Bruce put in many miles of river travel, praising God for the safety that he usually enjoyed. It was almost inevitable he would collide with something eventually.

The first time Bruce really hit a submerged rock, the 10 metre motorboat went right up onto the top of it. The propeller was under the water at first, but as the water level fell, the propeller was exposed and there was danger of the whole boat tipping over. Bruce had to climb out onto the rock and steady the heavy, ironwood-hulled boat while he waited for help to come.

Bruce had been given a plastic pith helmet as a joke, and he was wearing it. As he waited on the rock, steadying the boat, occasionally calling for help across the empty river, the pith helmet started to melt in the sun.

Four hours passed. Finally Bruce saw a canoe slowly round the bend, paddled by a Dayak whom he knew. This man stopped paddling and put the paddle across his knees. Bruce recalled much later, with a laugh, 'He didn't smile or anything. Even though it was so ludicrous, this great big white man, standing on the rock, holding this boat, with his helmet melting in the sun. He drifted opposite me, and asked, "Didn't you know there was a rock there?" '

The sight of the launch often galvanized the locals into suddenly needing to visit relatives up or downstream, so the boat was usually full of them, while Bruce steered and Annette tried to cook in the tiny galley and care for a very active Simon.

In a hurry to get home to Annette and the boys one night, Bruce decided to ignore everyone and thus sailed right past an army post that was signalling him to stop. Next day he received a severe dressing down for his disrespect (for which he apologized) and was grateful that nothing worse happened. (They were known to shoot!) He had learnt his lesson!

Once, Annette, having had a complete disaster of a morning – baby Simon scratchy, eleven interruptions (sick or not-so-sick folk) to her attempts to home-school Paul – let out all her frustration on an old Dayak man who had come long before the afternoon clinic opened, wanting of all things – worm medicine!

After rebuking him angrily, she fled to her bedroom and burst into tears. Re-emerging some time later, she found with relief that the old man was still squatting in the doorway, chewing his betel-nut, waiting patiently.

She asked him to forgive her, gave him a coffee, squatted beside him for a chat, then gave him the worm medicine. She had learnt her lesson, too!

31

It was typical of Bruce and Annette that the next step forward for the work of God in the Ketungau came not from careful planning, but out of Bruce's prayer room.

Humanly speaking, had Bruce not been 'watching and praying' – had he not been at his post – this work would have suffered a severe setback.

As it was, the first shots were fired of the most enormous battle of his life – the memory of which choked him with tears even as he recounted the story, thirty years later.

Most of the story happened after Bruce and Annette's first home leave (1973), but the first trouble began in 1971, not long after they'd moved to Nanga Merakai.

One morning, Bruce had an enormous urge to go to the Merakai church and offer to incorporate it officially under the WEC banner. Until then, Bruce had not cared what the little congregations were called.

That morning, he felt the command of the Spirit was so clear that he cancelled his plans for the day, gathered the elders together, and explained what he'd like to do.

They were enthusiastic – keen to be linked to an international Christian body. So they composed an official letter and all signed up to it.

An unexpected visitor arrived a few hours later. He was the representative of an older Indonesian denomination, and had set off from his church's headquarters in Pontianak fully a week before, hoping to sign up the Nanga Merakai church for his own organization! Bruce, following only his sense of leading from God, had pipped him by a few hours.

This was a lot more serious than it sounds. Bruce had heard that there were church groups in Indonesia who were eager to add to their numbers by signing up tribal people without ever insisting on a radical break with the old ways. The Western world has largely forgotten this, but there are some situations (Indonesia is one) where church office represents power, wealth and prestige, and denominations squabble like multinationals for market share.

This wouldn't be so bad if they were all preaching the gospel. But this group wasn't. Like the 'circumcision group' in the New Testament – opposed so bitterly by the apostles – they preached an emasculated version of the gospel that liberated no-one from sin or evil powers.

With so few of the 'Christians' in the Ketungau grasping even the basics of the gospel, Bruce and Annette sought God for the next step forward. They began to hold what they called 'lightning courses' at various central villages throughout the region, giving five days of intensive teaching, with gospel meetings in the evenings. (Paul enjoyed these times with lots of playmates, and his repertoire of sermons, Bible stories and choruses was later played out to his imaginary audience at home. Simon was happy anywhere, as long as he was fed!)

32

Not long before their home leave, Bruce and family, with Jonah, a young Christian Dayak, moored their canoe at a village called Two Fork River, left the outboard with the friendly village head and set off on the two-hour trek to a village where a small group of folk had 'entered the Lord's way'.

On the hill behind the village, they passed a grove of tall trees which, unusually, hadn't been cut down. Jonah explained that this grove of trees must be sacred. Sure enough, Jonah pointed to the ironwood idols in the middle of the grove, where the undergrowth had been cleared.

This provoked Bruce. 'Let's pray,' he said. They joined hands and Bruce prayed a simple prayer telling the evil spirits that in Jesus' authority he was putting a stop to their influence right now. They could no longer exercise authority in the area, blinding people to the truth of the gospel. They sang a chorus – the Indonesian version of the familiar *'In the name of Jesus, we have the victory.'* Then they carried on with their trek and thought no more of it.

Bruce and Annette returned from home leave to Nanga Merakai in September 1973. The next time Bruce dropped his canoe off at Two Fork River, the village headman asked him in for a coffee.

'Did you pray at our sacred grove?' He wasn't hostile, just curious.

'As a matter of fact, I did,' replied Bruce.

'I thought so. The spirits have gone. We went up there to make some offerings and they've all gone.'

Later still, Bruce heard that one of the trees had been struck by lightning, at which point the villagers decided that the trees were worth more as boards, so they cut them down. Two Fork village (which had previously not welcomed the gospel) invited Jonah to come and explain the Christian way.

33

The scene to which Bruce and Annette returned in 1973 was not the one into which they had chugged in the little houseboat in 1969. The Ketungau was no longer a Cold War frontier. The Indonesian Army was in control of the border areas, the guerrillas were no longer a problem, and the government was pouring development resources into the jungle, establishing schools in every central village and giving training to village leaders.

Bruce had more than fulfilled his goal of taking the gospel to every village, ably helped for eighteen months by the Timorese evangelists. This was a phenomenal achievement – hundreds of miles trekked through jungles or travelled by canoe and outboard; hundreds of nights spent in smoky longhouses, eating whatever food was served; hundreds of occasions where Jesus Christ and his salvation was presented to the Dayaks.

In 1969 few people in the Eastern Ketungau had made any kind of response to Jesus Christ. By 1973 many villages had made decisions to adopt the Christian way. Perhaps 7,000 of the Dayaks of the Eastern Ketungau were *Kristen Protestan* – or at least were registered that way to the satisfaction of the government statisticians.

These were still early days both in Bruce and Annette's missionary career and for the work of God in the Eastern Ketungau. Bruce and Annette themselves were still in the early stage of really getting to grips with Dayak culture, learning lots but making many mistakes. Spreading themselves over such an enormous area did not help build the kinds of relationships through which discipleship can be modelled. Nor did the animistic background of the Dayaks themselves, distrustful of everyone, lead them easily to open their hearts to Bruce and Annette.

The news from further north, where Adjuk and family with Yoktan had moved, was discouraging. Yoktan had exercised a remarkable ministry, seeing dramatic healings and miraculous acts of God which opened many doors to the Gospel. But he had returned home and Adjuk was not following up this fine work.

A pattern of unfaithfulness in small things had developed to bigger things. Later this would lead to Adjuk being removed from ministry and Bruce resuming responsibility for the Upper Ketungau, when already much that was promising had been lost. (Adjuk gradually returned to the old ways, becoming a feared and powerful occult practitioner. Thankfully, news from his family told of his repentance not long before his death.)

Throughout the region, the old ways still maintained their hold. The villagers who had signed up as Protestants had an extremely hazy knowledge of the new Christian way, and visits were too infrequent to build on the little they knew.

Sickness was a test that most failed. Infant deaths were common. Moving from a mindset that sickness was caused by the spirits was not easily done. With a sick child on your hands, pressure from the extended family, non-occult medicine seeming to have failed, what would any of us do if not turn to the received wisdom of our ancestors? When it came to illness, almost everyone tried anything for the sake of the child – *asal sembuh* (as long as they were healed).

Fear is the overriding characteristic of animism – fear of the spirits, fear of breaking the many *pantang* (taboos) and rules that offered protection against the spirits. So the ritual ceremonies in the cycle of life – for example when rice was planted or harvested – continued, the baskets for spirit offerings still hung from the roof, sacred trees or in a few cases the idols guarding a village entrance remained untouched because they could only be chopped down or destroyed if the whole village agreed.

Except for a few scattered groups, it was rare for the people in the Eastern Ketungau in 1973 to have made a clean break with the spirits.

In the realm of family life, it would be many years before the gospel would begin to make an impact: children were still shamed, scared and deceived into obedience, sometimes still cursed in the name of the spirits. It was normal to lie to children, to say anything to stop them crying. From their early years, girls were taught to be inconspicuous so as not to attract the attention of the spirits. Fear permeated family life.

A young man, failing to attract the attentions of a girl, might employ a *dukun* to put a spell on her. Such a *jayau,* which might sound like a fairytale to some Western ears, was neither a joke nor a fairytale in Dayak culture. It had power; it drove some girls mad, and was probably one of the causes of the madness of Bruce and Annette's former helper, Giah.

34

Annette's home-based ministry changed and expanded. She taught the Religious Education classes in both schools and led the Sunday School, the ladies' meeting and the youth group. Since Bruce was away much of the time, she helped teach at the Nanga Merakai church.

Each morning, except for Friday RE classes, Annette supervised Paul's schoolwork and each afternoon ran the medical clinic.

It was an exhausting and challenging time, yet for Annette, the privilege of sharing the truth where for centuries the Devil's lies had wielded control, made it more than worthwhile.

Gradually the young people took over the Sunday School, and a local RE teacher the primary school classes, but it would be 1975 before Margaret Price (from Australia) and soon after Janny Riemersma (from the Netherlands) joined them to share in the growing ministries.

Over the years, scores of high-schoolers found a living faith in Christ, and many of these maintained a fine Christian testimony into adulthood. Some became school teachers, government officials or nurses, and a number obtained university degrees.

Some of the Dayak boys who had been introduced to Christ in the 1950s by Isobel Stephenson and Gladys Rusha became the first evangelists and pastors. A few entered the CMA Bible college, becoming the first local leaders.

Jambi had made a genuine commitment to Christ in the school at Nanga Sekalau, but fell away. He had been restored to the Lord when his new-born baby daughter died at Annette's clinic and Bruce helped to bury her. Jambi became Bruce's companion on many of his treks and later a faithful elder in the Nanga Merakai church. He was also a tireless witness and evangelist.

Obed was another 'schoolboy' of Gladys', though he was not converted until he found himself in jail over in Sarawak. (His papers were not in order!)

Bruce and Annette had first met Obed back at Nanga Sekalau. He was paddling his tiny canoe down to the CMA Bible school to start his second year there, with nothing to his name beyond a spare set of clothes, a month's supply of rice and a burning call from God to preach the gospel. (He also, Annette diagnosed, had a bad dose of amoebic dysentery.)

It may not sound strange that he was paddling a canoe except that he came from one of the farthest villages in the Upper Ketungau and was returning to a Bible school on the banks of the Kapuas River far down river from Sintang. By motorboat, this trip would take 2-3 days; alone, paddling a canoe, at least a week to 10 days.

Bruce and Annette saw in Obed a supreme love for Christ, a determination to do His will, and an integrity that marked him out as extraordinary among the believers. Yet he was a typically gentle and self-effacing Dayak. That day at Nanga Sekalau, he scrubbed their pots in the Ketungau River until they shone – even though he was weakened by dysentery, and washing pots was not one of the chores that Dayak men usually did.

Later they learnt that he refused to ask for financial help at the Bible school, wanting to prove God in the midst of poverty and need. The staff at the CMA college, missionary and national alike, spoke highly of him. Obed graduated with his faith strong and the call of God evident on his life, and he played an important role in the newly-forming church structures.

35

By 1975 the expatriate team was growing and, alongside a few Bible-trained Dayak evangelists, began to enter the long-neglected WEC areas – Norma Hunt was already established in the Upper Lebang area; Australian Joan Campbell joined the Woodwards at the Nanga Lebang headquarters; Myrtle Whitehead from New Zealand, who first entered West Kalimantan in 1950, then served in Java for many years, returned to the Kantuk (Iban) area that she had pioneered in the

1950s. Aussie Ken 'KJ' Jordin joined the team to build much needed airstrips – and did much more.

Canadian Mike Shumik, and later with his English wife Barbara, was responsible for the Suruk area of the vast Upper Kapuas, pioneered by Obed; Aussies John and Rosemary Callaghan worked in the upper Silat, replaced on their return home by Peter and Rae Smith, also from Australia. All of these couples had small children, and proved God's provision and protection in very isolated situations.

New Zealanders Ken and Colleen Ward moved to the Upper Ketungau, later replaced by Americans David and Judy Phillips, thus removing the heavy responsibility of supervision from Bruce's shoulders. Margaret Price and Janny Riemersma made excellent contributions not only to the ministry at Nanga Merakai but further afield. Rex and Beryl Gray, from Australia, settled in the upper Sekalau, Rex also using his gifts in producing training materials.

Only longer-term workers have been named, but each worker played a vital role in the planting and building of the church in the vast areas of the WEC work.

36

The 'lightning courses' were only a temporary solution but blessed of God. Obed urged them to start a simple lay-leaders' training programme for the whole of the work. Obed's burden gelled with Bruce and Annette's and the concept of a KKS (Lay

Leadership Training Course) was formed.

In 1975 this idea was accepted by the team (after being initially turned down). So the KKS was born, modelled on a successful course run in West Irian among illiterate tribal peoples. Set up at Nanga Merakai, it ran for a month during May and November, the slack times of the rice-growing season.

The first module of the course began in May 1976 with Margaret Price helping. From then on at least two of the six modules ran simultaneously, with both nationals and missionaries teaching the Bible and 'How To' subjects, as well as simple lessons on health and Christian family. Each weekend, teams of two went out to the villages to put into practice what they had learnt.

Scores of men (and some women) completed at least a few of the modules during the six years the courses ran and seven men graduated from the complete course, among them Jonah. Many of the participants became local church leaders and four of them are still pastors in the national church.

All these advances had their challenges. Family life was a huge one, with Simon suffering many accidents until Bruce and Annette took a definite stand of faith for his health and wellbeing. The biggest conflict, however, was with the Indonesian denomination that was trying to take over their work.

37

One morning as he was praying in the houseboat, Bruce had a sudden premonition that something was going to happen that day.

Not long after, he heard the impressive 40 hp roar of a large speedboat coming up the river. In it was a minister from Sintang and a leader of their church synod all the way from Pontianak – the same man who had earlier tried to sign up the Nanga Merakai church.

They eased off the engine outside Bruce and Annette's house, guided the boat to the wooden raft, moored it, and walked up the path. Bruce met them and invited them in while Annette served coffee.

They talked, and Bruce realized that they were delivering an ultimatum: we are moving into your patch.

'But the Governor has specifically forbidden you to do this,' Bruce told them.

'Oh, we don't worry too much about that.' The Christian movement pioneered by Bruce and Annette was too tempting a target to overlook.

Bruce went on. 'I can hear you talking about gathering Dayaks under your banner, and I hear a lot about how good it is to have an Indonesian denomination with no foreigners, but I don't hear you talking much about the Dayaks turning away from sin, breaking with the spirits, and being converted to live a new life. I don't hear much about repentance and faith in Christ!'

The sad truth was that this denomination had fallen away from the gospel, and had degenerated into power politics and to spreading its influence through persuading and bribing the people. Often, they specifically targeted leaders who had fallen away. There was a cynicism at the heart of what they were doing that made Bruce indignant.

'Do you mean to say,' – Bruce was angry now, one of the very few times that Annette could ever remember such a word being appropriate for Bruce – 'You come here and think you can joke and toy with people's souls?'

After they left, Bruce realized with mounting alarm what this would mean. The Christian movement in the hands of this denomination had never matured beyond that initial group turning. If they took over in the Eastern Ketungau, the same would happen here.

Bruce began to pray. He would go down to the quiet of the houseboat and seek the Lord, hour after hour. As he prayed, the realization deepened that this group was really a deadly threat.

Who could blame the Dayaks if they joined a denomination that seemed to offer everything a religion had to give, but allowed them to keep their old ways – using their witchdoctors, sacrificing to the spirits, holding their feasts?

It looked hopeless though. This rival denomination was Indonesian, its synod based in Kalimantan, so could claim to be a true Dayak denomination. They made much of Bruce, a foreigner, planting a 'Western denomination'. And they were offering what looked like a much easier version of the Christian faith.

One of the Timorese evangelists went to visit this denomination's minister in Sintang. He was told: 'What are you doing working for this foreigner? We are going to sweep your little church into the river!'

So Bruce prayed, morning after morning, sometimes with others, but mostly on his own. 'Lord, this church is a threat to your baby church all across the Ketungau. I want you to clear them out of here so that your gospel can go forward.'

This little prayer became a burden to him like a backpack that he couldn't take off. Sometimes he went to the houseboat at noon as well; and sometimes, late into the night.

He grew bolder. He remembered the parable of the friend who asked another friend for three loaves of bread and he became equally determined to ask for a specific thing, and not to give up until he got it.

Again and again he would take himself to the houseboat, open the Bible at the parable of the importunate friend, put his finger on the passage, and say, 'Here I am again Lord! You know what I'm going to ask you for. I'm going to keep on asking you until I know you've answered. I want you to clear that group out of here so that your gospel can go forward.'

Years later Bruce remembered, tears streaming down his face, 'I think God was pleased with that prayer. In fact I know he was.'

38

About a month after that initial visit, Bruce heard over the grapevine that a schoolteacher in the Upper Ketangau area had invited the minister from Sintang to come up to their village church. Bruce knew that this schoolteacher was corrupt and keen to take every opportunity for outward advance with as little inward change as possible. He had influenced a small group of people in the village to think the same way.

The following Sunday morning, Bruce saw the Sintang minister's boat powering up the river while he was standing on the veranda about to go to church.

Bruce was agitated all through the service. When it was over, he told Annette that he was going to try to catch up with this minister, and limit the damage. He hastily packed and set off in the motorboat.

All through the day he chugged up the river, moored the motorboat at a village and spent the night in the boat. After tossing and turning for hours, praying and wondering what to do, he deliberately handed over his worries to the Lord and fell asleep.

The next day he set off early. From that village, the dark Ketungau River made a huge arc. He planned to take a short-cut, a thirty-mile hike through the jungle – the trek of his life.

Bruce was still extremely fit from his farming, wood-chopping, Aussie Rules days and from years of trekking. He was known as a man who could out-walk any missionary and any Dayak. It is doubtful that anyone could have kept pace with him that day.

He didn't know the way. He kept getting lost. At one point he rushed too hastily across a tree-trunk bridge, and fell right into the river. Dragging himself ruefully out, he realized his pack now weighed twice as much and who knows what was happening to the new trousers he had packed for the meetings!

He arrived in the early evening. Ignoring the schoolteacher and his group, Bruce went to the church leader's house, where he was welcomed, and invited to preach at the meeting that night.

He had a bath, a quick meal and a lie-down, got changed into his fresh clothes – the trousers had shrunk – and was calmly sitting in the congregation when the minister from Sintang walked in.

The minister was so astonished that he didn't dare to try to sheep-steal that night. Bruce preached, in his shrunken trousers, inwardly laughing and feeling the Lord was smiling too.

The minister from Sintang suggested a second meeting the following day. Bruce couldn't do anything about this: someone in the village had invited him, after all.

So the next morning, Bruce went off to visit another village, with the church elder coming part of the way to show him the path.

Before the elder returned home, Bruce suggested that they prayed. They knelt down in the grass next to the muddy path. Bruce was still burning with indignation at the way this minister was cutting in on the work of God. But even Bruce was surprised at what came out of his own mouth: 'In the Name of the Lord Jesus Christ,' he prayed, 'I shut his mouth, this minister from Sintang, and I command that he will not be able to utter one word which shall in any way cause this baby church to stumble.'

So he went on to the village and stayed the night. Next day, when he returned, he asked at the police post about the previous night's meeting. The policeman started to laugh.

'You wouldn't believe it! The minister walked out to the front like someone in a daze and looked up at the ceiling, looked around, opened his mouth and said nothing. Not a word came out.

'So he went back and sat down again. They sang another verse of a hymn, and he came out again, and nothing happened. So they had to sing again. The third time he came out, he gave a message about rejoicing in the Lord always.'

One little battle was won but the conflict continued for years. For Bruce it was an entirely spiritual problem, and there were no shades of grey: an attempt by Satan to neutralize a large section of God's work.

On he prayed. It could have seemed pointless – a solitary man in his boat, talking to God, the work of God in the Eastern Ketungau in the balance. Bruce didn't care. These were holy times.

One morning, Bruce woke up in a village where he had preached the previous night. He had a strong urge to get alone with God. It took a little effort to detach himself from the villagers but finally he found an old schoolroom and took himself to prayer.

Thumbing through his Bible he came to Zechariah 4:7 which, in Bruce's English version read,

'Who art thou, O thou great mountain? Before Zerubbabel thou shalt become a plain.'

Somehow that obscure verse gripped Bruce's heart as the answer he had been waiting for. He knew God had heard him. From that day he didn't ask any more that this denomination would be cast out of the area. He just praised God, and waited for him to do it.

39

Lidung was only two hours from Nanga Merakai. Bruce had been making regular trips and was trusting the Lord to do something powerful which would be a further stepping stone into that whole area of the Sekapat.

This longhouse had a powerful *manang* called Pak Serani. (A *manang* is the person in charge of the village rituals – a kind of priest figure.)

Most of the witchdoctors in the area were his former pupils. He was a little man and would probably have stood full height underneath Bruce's arm. He was very well known and effective. He didn't like Bruce, and when Bruce would come to take a meeting, Serani would walk up and down the long veranda beating a gong the whole time!

One night in Lidung a man from Nanga Merakai called Tugik asked Bruce if he would pray for his older sister who was very ill. He took Bruce to see her. She was in the last stages of what looked like tuberculosis, just a bag of bones.

'Not only could you count every rib,' Bruce later remembered, 'but you could almost put your fingers between them. She was absolutely emaciated. She couldn't lie down because she would go into a paroxysm of coughing, so she sat leaning on a kerosene tin, on which was a filthy pillow.'

Tugik said, 'I want you to pray for her.' But the other family members would not give permission, because they wanted to consult Serani the witchdoctor first.

'As the night wore on,' Bruce remembered, 'it developed into a confrontation between the witchdoctor and me, but of course it was an encounter between the Lord Jesus and Satan.

After a couple of hours, Tugik came back and said, 'No, they haven't made up their minds yet.' Then later he reported that they said, 'We'll use the witchdoctor again, but if she's not any better then you can pray for her.'

Bruce said, 'No way! This is a confrontation between the power of the Lord Jesus Christ and the power of Satan. Tell them they have to make up their minds. If they're going to use the witchdoctor, I will not pray for her. If they decide not to use the witchdoctor I will pray for her.'

It may have been about midnight when Tugik finally came out after a long discussion and said, 'Over to you.'

Bruce's faith was small. He admitted afterwards that he prayed for her only because this confrontation had arisen and he believed he was being obedient to God.

Next morning they decided to take her to Annette's clinic. She couldn't lie down, so they seated her on a chair tied to a man's back. Finally they arrived at the clinic. Annette – Bruce remembered – was horrified.

'Bruce,' she scolded, 'why have you brought this poor woman to me in this condition?'

Looking a little like a guilty schoolboy, Bruce told her, 'Darling, the Lord led me to pray for her last night, so I did.'

Medicine was going to be useless: it would have to be the

Lord who healed. Annette gave her something to help her laboured breathing, then the family took her to Tugik's house with instructions to come back after the weekend.

When the clinic opened on Monday, Annette was still inside getting her medicines ready, while Bruce went out on the veranda to chat with the folk waiting.

He noticed a very thin lady, shabbily dressed, with a big grin on her face. She had walked slowly up from the river, climbed the front steps and was sitting on the veranda.

'Where do you come from?' he asked.

'From Lidung. You remember me!'

Bruce decided to be 'Indonesian' and replied, 'Well, I do remember you, but I can't remember exactly where I met you.'

'I'm the lady you prayed for.'

'No!' Bruce quickly called Annette.

'Do you recognise this woman?' Annette looked at her for a long time and said, 'No, I don't.'

'She's the lady from Lidung, the one we brought up in the canoe on Friday.'

After minimal treatment, she returned home perfectly well and went back working in the rice field. Bruce recalled, 'Everybody acknowledged it was a miracle that God had done. You couldn't say anything else.'

When Serani, the old *manang* saw this, he said, 'The Lord has more power than I have.'

So, he contacted Bruce's trekking partner, Jambi, and said, 'Jambi, I want you to come down on Sunday afternoon; bring the *pendeta* (minister). I want to burn all my fetishes and my occult objects.' He had piles of them.

Bruce remembered: 'So we went down. He brought out all of his paraphernalia, while the folk stood around, laughing a little as Dayaks do when they are anxious or embarrassed. We made a big fire. We tried to burn those things and even though they'd been in his room, and close to the fire (they must have been tinder-dry), some of them were almost impossible to burn.

The Dayaks had told me that if you try to burn something that has occult power the fire won't burn it. I didn't believe them then, but I do now. I had to get a machete and split some of those wooden idols into small pieces before they would burn. Then we counselled Serani. He spoke little Indonesian so Jambi counselled him and I added anything that I felt wasn't clear. This old fellow made a clear-cut stand for Christ.'

Jambi visited him regularly, and Serani often came to the Rattrays' house, always with some fish and a big, toothless betel-nut smile.

40

Over the years, this passion for sharing the gospel and taking every opportunity to do so made an unforgettable impact on the boy who had wondered if his daddy loved the Dayaks more than him. Paul, who now has the same passion as his dad, recalled one of his first treks with him to a remote village in the upper Sekalau: 'It was the durian season, so everyone but the very old were camped high in the hills waiting for the durian to fall.'

Durian is a delicacy amongst the Dayak, in fact, it is so highly valued that the Dayak build huts in the forest under durian trees so they can be the first to pick up the falling fruit. Durian trees are tall, often standing over 60 metres high. Falling from this height, the spiky fruit can kill or maim, so Dayaks build the huts reinforced with thick bark roofs to protect them from the falling fruit.

'After walking along narrow, steep tracks for nearly an hour in fading light, we saw the lights of a number of huts under a stand of giant durian trees.

'Dad asked to speak to the headman, who reluctantly agreed to call all he could to a meeting that night. Because durian mainly fall in the cool of night, usually when a wind blows, getting a group of Dayak spread over a few square kilometres of hill country to come to an evening meeting was a challenge.

'After nearly two hours the headman returned with a small group of Dayak men, women and children. Dad shared a simple gospel message with the sound of durian falling around us and people regularly leaving the meeting to find the fruit.

'I learnt a valuable lesson from, and about, Dad that night. No matter what the circumstances, you always take the opportunity to share the gospel.'

41

Bruce hired men, mostly from a village downriver, to build an airstrip, greatly enjoying the manual work and getting burnt by the sun darker than any of them.

One day he told his work team, 'Look guys, I want you to fell all the trees wider than the airstrip, right through the distance here for about 750 metres, so the plane can glide in.'

Then he left for a few days of ministry. When he returned, he looked at what they had cleared.

Enjoying himself, he said, 'If my eyes don't deceive me, I can see a big tree right in the middle of the approach to the airstrip. Am I seeing right?'

Smiling back, they replied, 'You are.'

'Would you mind telling me why that is there? The plane can't come in – it's right plumb in the middle.'

'We left that tree there because it has *naneng*.'

'What's *naneng*?' Bruce asked.

'It's a little animal.'

'What do you mean, a little animal? How big is it?'

'Oh, about that long.' They showed a length about 4 cm.

'What colour is it?'

'It has gold and black stripes on it.'

'What does it do?'

'Oh, it flies and it stings.'

'Do you mean to tell me that you grown men will let a little animal about 4 cm long keep you from felling a tree that's going to stop a plane from landing! I don't believe it!'

'Well,' they replied, 'we're not going to go up there. It's a nest of *naneng*. If we try to fell that tree they will sting us; it's really painful and we'll pass out.'

'Is there anyone here brave enough to come with me after lunch and fell that tree?'

Only one was, a witchdoctor from another village.

But after lunch the Dayaks insisted, 'Don't do it! They'll sting you! They'll drive you mad!'

'Ah come on! You're grown men!'

So Bruce and the witchdoctor, plus Scamp, went to attack the tree. Scamp stuck his nose straight in the hole, was stung and fled howling from the scene to nurse his rapidly-swelling muzzle.

Bruce got out his axe and walloped the tree about four times until the witchdoctor yelled out, 'Look out! Here they come!'

Bruce stopped while the wasps buzzed and dive-bombed him from all directions. He waited until they calmed down, then attacked the tree again. This time, they came at him like a squadron of fighter planes.

Bruce remembered, 'They got in my hair, and inside my shirt, and stung like nothing I'd ever felt before. You could feel the sting going numb as soon as it entered. I must have had eight stings. So I decided that discretion is the better part of valour and we left the wasps to their tree.

'When I got back to the hill again, the guys were all there looking down, and one of them said to me,

'"If my eyes don't deceive me, you know, I could swear that tree's still there. What happened?"

'I said, "Ah, it's a bit too hot today. I thought maybe we'd leave it until tomorrow."

'I showed them some of the stings. "No, you won't," they replied. "Tomorrow you'll be feverish from the stings."

'I was too! What the men did in the end was light a fire under it at night and then chop it down.'

The airstrip allowed Mission Aviation Fellowship's (MAF's) little Cessna planes to land a half-hour from Nanga Merakai instead of a day's journey away at Nanga Lebang. They had an unforgettable opening day, with several Dayaks riding up in the plane. Among other things, it enabled Paul to fly the 70-minute flight to and from the International School near the west coast where he boarded.

42

Samsia (known as Sam) was a lovely young woman from a Malay people group called the Serawai on the Indonesian island of Sumatra, over 1000 miles from Kalimantan.

A large number of Serawai had come to Christ, the only people movement ever among the Muslim Malays.

Sam had attended Bible School and come to Kalimantan as a co-worker of a new WEC missionary named Colleen. She worked in the Upper Merakai and after Colleen left, became like a daughter to the Rattrays.

Nanga Merakai's primary school had a Dayak head teacher, Pak Robin, who in due course fell in love with Sam and approached her about marriage. Culture required parental consent obtained through a third party. Bruce and Annette were the third party in her case, so Robin had to come and be 'looked over' by Bruce.

Robin was from the CMA area to the west, where many were second generation Christians. Bruce pressed him about whether he knew Christ personally and, although Robin gave all the right answers, still Bruce and Annette wondered. Yet they knew Robin to be a fine man and involved in the church, so they agreed to the engagement.

Sam's home church in Sumatra was not at all in agreement. They felt it was a very big step down for her to be marrying a Dayak (although Robin was actually better educated than she was), who was also not a Christian worker. So Sam went home to visit her family and church, carrying a letter of recommendation from the mission.

A few weeks later, a visibly-distressed Sam returned to Nanga Merakai and explained what had happened.

Her parents were believers but illiterate. Sam's married brother was still a Muslim and he determined to thwart this marriage. He had a particular man in mind for her, and when Sam would visit her brother, this man was sure to be there. When her brother brought the man around to Sam's home, she would say, 'I don't want to see him,' and she wouldn't come out of her room.

Then Sam's brother apparently arranged to have a spell put on her. Even though Sam was a godly young woman, this spell had a powerful effect. She would be overcome with an uncontrollable desire to go to this Muslim man (even though she could not stand the sight of him before this). She would pray, but latterly she was finding it increasingly hard to pray. In desperation, she asked her parents to lock her in her room at these times, and not let her out, even though she pleaded with them or even tried to break down the door.

Sam was alone; her church, because of in-fighting, carelessly unaware of her need. She became ill and no-one knew what was wrong with her. She ended up in the local hospital.

It's hard to know what would have happened to Sam, had not Ruth Loan visited her. Ruth was a WEC missionary who had worked in that area of Sumatra for many years and knew Sam. She prayed for her and the curse was broken. When Sam left the hospital, she made immediate arrangements to return to Kalimantan.

Sam's experience in Sumatra shocked Bruce and Annette but reinforced to them an important spiritual principle – the responsibility of leadership towards the vulnerable. Sam should not have been affected by the curse, but she was in a spiritually hostile environment, and the church, which should have been a kind of umbrella for her, was so busy bickering that they gave her no cover at all. This small town church later split and many more were stumbled by it.

It was a wonderful day in June 1975 when Sam and Robin were married. They were a valuable couple, later taking over the youth work at Nanga Merakai. Robin proved to be a faithful husband and church elder. Some years later he was transferred to Sintang, where he became Head of Personnel for Education.

Robin had a vision for young Dayak men to take their place in the development of the interior and worked hard to see that happen. This vision was later realised with a number of important positions being filled by young men Robin had mentored.

The day before Robin and Sam's wedding, while Bruce was away collecting guests, Annette received the news that Bruce's dad, Warren, had died suddenly of a heart attack five days before.

Bruce was in shock for some time. He felt the lack of his father's prayers as much as a soldier on the front line feels it when the artillery behind him falls silent. He realized he had to reorder his own priorities to spend even more time alone with God.

43

All this time Bruce was carrying with him God's promise that the rival denomination would be cleared right out of the area – the 'mountain' of their presence would become a plain.

Bruce was confident in the promise of God. But on the ground, the situation got much worse. The minister from Sintang wrote to the Governor of West Kalimantan and army officials, explaining that Bruce was obstructing an indigenous Indonesian work. (The Governor, although a Muslim, knew Bruce, and he wouldn't hear of it.) This minister then went up to another village in the Upper Ketungau, where one of the national workers was preparing a group of people for baptism, and baptized them all himself into his church.

Then he posted a church worker right in Nanga Merakai. The man visited the villages where Bruce had started churches. He took a bottle of whisky with him, offering it around the village, urging people to sign up with his denomination. Not one of the congregations took up the offer: Dayaks might have been illiterate but they could read people. After a few months, the man gave up and quietly, at night, left the area.

Still Bruce waited for God to act, going down to the boat each morning, praising him for the deliverance that was going to happen.

In 1976, the loose arrangement of WEC missionaries and national believers who had been meeting together as a WEC-related church body became an official Indonesian denomination, GPSK (the Fellowship of Christ's Church). It was led by eight Dayaks and four expatriates, the Dayaks being keen to have the foreigners in the leadership team, insisting that 'they were Dayaks too.' They also needed the ex-pats' experience and expertise in those early years.

Obed was appointed the first leader of this official denomination, and Bruce was his deputy. They had come to the decision to form a denomination after a lot of prayer, partly because of government requirements, and partly as a response to the continuing pressure from the rival church.

44

In the midst of all this, Bruce and Annette were still seeing some astonishing miracles, as bound-up lives were unlocked and freed.

Maryam was a professing Christian, married with a teenage family, but in great need. When she came to Bruce and Annette for help, they were at first reluctant to receive her, stretched to the limit as they were with local commitments and preparing for the next KKS training course. They sensed she would need a lot of prayer and counsel. But they also knew that if they refused, she would likely turn to the medicine men, whose attempted cures would lead to deeper satanic bondage and probable insanity. Only Christ could heal Maryam.

The first couple of weeks were hard work. Maryam could not bear to be alone and followed Annette constantly. At night, she would be woken by hearing voices and seeing ugly, demonic visions. From the beginning, Bruce and Annette, applying their authority in Christ, deliberately bound the demon powers in her and led her in a verbal prayer, sentence by sentence, renouncing all ground she may have given to Satan, consciously or unconsciously.

Maryam started to improve, and they were able to give simple Bible teaching on Christ's forgiveness and victory over the enemy. They praised and worshipped God together which seemed to help her as much as anything.

Then things started to slide again. Maryam told them that as they prayed, demon powers would pinch and hit her. They counselled her to ask the Holy Spirit to reveal to her the ground in her life which allowed the demons to remain. She had been 'surrendered' to two powerful *manang* as a child and had used scores of *dukun* since. She asked for forgiveness and cleansing as the Holy Spirit brought them to mind.

This seemed to really stir things up. 'If you keep this up, you will die!' the voices kept telling her. The Rattrays reassured her. 'Not you, them, for they will have to go.' She found increasing deliverance, often confessing the names of several *dukun* in a single day.

After spending a few days with her sister, and having some doubtful 'treatments', she seemed to run into a wall, with no further progress. She began to show symptoms of mental instability, often confused or smiling as at some private joke.

Bruce and Annette made this a definite matter of prayer over the next few days. There was an added urgency, because Bruce was due to fly out to speak at a CMA national church conference. They must break through before he left.

The day before he left, Annette awoke with the distinct impression that there were two demons still there. When she shared this with Bruce, it confirmed an impression he had received too. After carefully explaining this to Maryam, Bruce commanded these two to give their names. One gave his name to her as 'Madness' and was cast out, followed soon afterwards by another called 'Powerful'.

And suddenly, she was completely free. Annette recalled, 'What a wonderful sense of the Lord's presence filled the room that morning as we triumphantly sang our chorus together, "Let's just praise the Lord!" It seemed that the angels joined together with us!

'No need now for someone to be with her. No need for medication to help her sleep. She read the Bible and sang hymns constantly, occasionally asking us to pray with her as the Holy Spirit brought to her mind unconfessed sins, even as far back as early childhood.

'Everyone who came in contact with her was blessed and challenged by her radiant testimony of love and gratitude to the

Lord. She stayed on for the KKS to care for the children and was a decided asset to the team.'

Not long after this healing, Annette received a letter from Maryam's sister. This woman was married to the head of local government, a Javanese Muslim, and she had been totally opposed to Maryam receiving any ministry from Bruce and Annette.

'Dear Mrs Rattray,' she wrote, 'I wish to open my heart to you. I have witnessed through the deliverance of my sister, Maryam, of whom it could almost be said, has been raised from the dead, by the power of God's Spirit. I just want you to know that I give all the glory to the Lord!'

45

Bruce was a passionate believer in prayer as a core, ingrained habit of life. He daily prayed for Annette, for their boys, for their national and missionary co-workers and for the growing Dayak family of believers. He systematically prayed for each village in the whole area. Annette and the boys used to joke that even an earthquake would not have dislodged him from his times in the Word and prayer.

Margaret, their close colleague at Merakai, wrote about this time, 'Bruce's prayer life was so powerful. I can still hear him now (Bruce had a loud voice) in his prayer hut at the back near my house – walking Kalimantan in prayer, covering each village, crying out to God for their salvation and for ways to reach them with the gospel. Then praying for his team; he prayed for each of us and desired the very best for us, praying that we would be God's instruments in reaching the Dayaks for Christ.'

Bruce's prayer life left an indelible impression upon their boys. Simon shares, 'One morning I went to Dad's study to call him for breakfast. I would usually run through the house making quite a racket, but as I approached his room, something stopped me from calling him. I tiptoed slowly toward the door. It sounded like he was talking to someone. I stopped to listen. I couldn't make out his words but I knew he was praying. It was then I felt a warm glow coming from the room. It is hard to describe, but it was like the Lord was there.'

Bruce and Annette with their co-workers, Margaret and Janny, began a weekly prayer time on a Wednesday afternoon. Some of the deacons from the Nanga Merakai church would join them after their day's work at the district government office or the school.

Later, they initiated a monthly day of prayer and other members of the widely scattered WEC team also began to set aside this time – the first Wednesday of the month.

Bruce and Annette also prayed what they called 'covenant prayers'. Here, they would agree to 'meet' someone regularly at a set time (often they were days' travel apart) with the specific aim of praying for the repentance of a husband, the return of some wayward child or another pressing need.

One example of such prayer was between Annette and Lon, a beautiful Dayak girl with an unfaithful rascal of a husband. Some 20 years after they started praying, Annette received a letter from Lon, saying, 'Praise God, Mama, and thank you for praying with me over the years. God has answered our Wednesday prayers and my husband has repented!'

46

The evident response of the ladies at Nanga Merakai to regular teaching on the Christian family had stirred their husbands to ask for a seminar. At first Bruce baulked. This was right out of his realm! Yet they had asked – most of them, men who he knew were only nominal Christians with a poor record as family men.

So with much trepidation, Bruce agreed, and the first Christian Family seminar was held. Bruce taught the Biblical principles and Annette the practical aspects, sharing honestly their own struggles and failures. It was so well received that an immediate request was made for another one the following year.

Bruce told them frankly, 'I have shared with you all I know!'

'Then teach it again' they said. 'We haven't taken it all in yet!'

The seminar was an important milestone not only for the Merakai church but also for Bruce. It was his first (and very reluctant) attempt at dealing with families and was the beginning of an enriched ministry for both of them. Without it and the vulnerability Bruce showed to the Merakai men, he and Annette would not have had the open homes and hearts they were privileged to enter and minister to then and in the following years.

Life was not 'all work and no play' though, and Bruce's irrepressible sense of humour made for lots of laughs for Annette and the boys and for Margaret and Janny who lived in a duplex near them. 'Blondy', their gibbon monkey, with her own brand of fun, added to the hilarity, though her antics were not always appreciated. Also she was a thief!

47

The World Council of Churches hosted a meeting at a large church in Pontianak, to which all the churches, Christian groups and government officials were invited. Obed and Bruce took the long journey to the coast as the WEC-related church delegation.

They found themselves sitting directly opposite the representatives from the opposing denomination, and these men lost no time in making their point at the meeting.

'We don't need foreigners here!' One of them had stood up and looked pointedly at Bruce. 'The Indonesian church should be for Indonesians only.'

But the leader of the meeting replied calmly, 'If a national church wants to choose Westerners as part of its leadership, we have no problem with that.'

The keynote address was given by the military governor of West Kalimantan, Bruce's friend from his days as military commander in the Ketungau during the Communist insurgency. He had taken a keen interest in Bruce's work ever since.

Although a Muslim and a Javanese, he was plain and direct. He looked at the other church and said, 'If Pak Rattray is ministering in an area and the folk have joined his group, it is not right for another church to go in there and try and take over his work. You go where no-one else is working.'

It was a message that was public, clear, unequivocal, and from the top, and at that conference the matter was finally put to rest. The other denomination had to withdraw. It was over.

Except for what Bruce, delightedly, called the 'icing on the cake'. He was picked as the keynote speaker at the joint celebration service when the convention was over. The minister of the church that hosted the gathering enjoyed his message so much, he asked Bruce to preach again at his church the following day, Sunday.

To fulfil this appointment, Bruce had to quickly locate a jacket and tie, as this traditional city church was quite formal. Bruce's jacket was in Australia and no-one else was his size. Happily he ran into an enormous Texan missionary down from the country, who kept a jacket and tie at his mission's headquarters. So Bruce preached, for perhaps the only time, in clothes that were actually too big for him. Courtesy of Radio Indonesia, Bruce's message was broadcast all over West Kalimantan.

BIBLE SCHOOL

48

In 1980, Bruce and Annette were asked to make perhaps the biggest sacrifice they had ever made – to leave Nanga Merakai and the Ketungau area.

It happened like this. Four years earlier, Bruce and Annette had been elected leaders of the WEC team, replacing Iain and Margaret Mackenzie, who had returned to the UK for their children's education.

With leadership came responsibilities that meant curtailing the large ministry they had in the Ketungau. As well as tackling extra administration, they needed to visit team members across the very large WEC area. Some of the team felt that the Rattrays would do this better if they moved away from the Ketungau, down to the mission headquarters at Nanga Lebang.

Then there was pressure from Obed and others in GPSK for WEC to help them set up a proper residential training programme for church leaders. The WEC team preferred to stick with the modular training that kept people in their own villages most of the year. But eventually Obed and the church prevailed. It was agreed to set up a Bible college with Obed as its principal and Bruce as deputy.

Then the painful blow for Bruce and Annette fell when the church council, nationals and missionaries together, not without some wrangling, decided to site the new Bible school at Nanga

Lebang and not at Nanga Merakai. The latter was favoured by the nationals because of its booming development, its rubber plantation for the students to work, and the accessibility to a large number of villages.

Nanga Lebang was central to the geography of the whole WEC area, but not strategic in any other way. Low-lying and hot, it lacked a concentration of villages nearby. It was even situated on a U-bend in the great Kapuas River on the wrong side of a short-cut used in high water; there was no short-cut to Nanga Lebang!

Compared with Nanga Merakai – with its thriving church, little parade of shops, government offices and secondary school filled with bright young students – it was a swamp.

Leaving Nanga Merakai and the Ketungau would mean the end of an era. Bruce's presence among the Dayaks of the Ketungau was large. He was the pioneering figure, the spiritual father of the movement. Even the true stories about him were larger than life (and there were many more colourful versions told in the villages).

He could fell four trees to their one, and he really did eat eight large durians at one sitting, in response to a village challenge.

He once sneezed so hard that his top set of false teeth shot out of his mouth and flew over the side of the boat, splashing into the flooded Kapuas River like an artillery shell. Iain Mackenzie, who was driving at the time, sighed and said, 'Och, the awful sense of finality!'

As we have seen, Bruce could out-walk any local or foreigner on a trail. He was tough and resourceful in a crisis and had a farmer's intense practicality and good sense.

He had cast out demons from people and prayed for the sick and seen them restored to full health. Through prayer he had once stopped a fire from destroying the rubber plantation on the Nanga Merakai property. Despite much opposition, he had been the instrument God had used to bring about the initial change in direction for many of the Dayaks of the Eastern Ketungau area.

It was not surprising that he came to be seen as the man with all the answers. And so Bruce had to face the hardest moment a person can face when God has done a good work through you – to leave that work behind.

Leaving behind the home their boys had grown up in, and their close relationships with some of the Merakai families, was a big wrench for all of them. An incident a few years before illustrated the affection of those families for the boys (and for Bruce and Annette).

Annette recalled, 'each year my parents sent Paul and Simon a Christmas parcel. We only received mail every 6-8 weeks if we went downriver. Christmas was just days away, so it was obvious the boys would miss out.

'We had asked the Lord to do a miracle, but there wasn't much faith in our prayers. I went down to our little bazaar, bought some things to wrap and put them under the small beringin tree (like a fine pine) that Bruce had cut down.

'The day before Christmas a canoe slid into the bank. Pak Wally, one of the deacons of the Merakai church, stepped out holding a large parcel. We could hardly believe our eyes!

'Pak Wally had been in Sintang with little expectation of getting home for Christmas because no more trading boats were coming upriver. But when he went to the post office to collect mail and saw the parcel, he knew he had to get it to the boys. That dear man borrowed a canoe and paddled upriver for five days just to bring that Christmas parcel for our boys. Boy, were we humbled!'

49

The fateful day came in April 1981, when Bruce, Annette, Paul and Simon packed up their things and piloted the small houseboat to Nanga Lebang, where several fine buildings had been erected by Peter Smith and some local workmen to house the new Bible school.

Bruce and Annette did so in submission to their team and to the church, but with deeply grieving hearts; not agreeing with the decision but accepting it as from God. Every 'death' experience, when embraced, brings forth life. They knew this would be so in the years ahead, but it did not make the experience any easier.

Bruce and Annette also grieved for their sons who found this move from their idyllic home almost as difficult, especially Paul, then almost 16. He was leaving not only a large group of teenage friends (Nanga Lebang had none except the new students) but his hunting companions – the older men, including Pak Wally, who from his early years had taught him the many skills he had mastered as a Dayak. In Indonesia you are supposed to register a move with the authorities. Bruce never did register this particular relocation. His body moved to Nanga Lebang: but he left his heart in the Ketungau.

With their customary enthusiasm, Bruce and Annette applied themselves to the new task.

The Antioch Bible School (SAA) opened in August 1981 with 12 students. All had completed at least two of the KKS (lay training course) modules.

The school was set up on the same lines as the WEC-related Indonesian Missionary Fellowship (IMF) Bible Institute in Java. This remarkable institution was in turn modelled on WEC's missionary training colleges, like the one in Tasmania where Bruce and Annette had been on staff while they awaited their visa.

Staff and students ate together, prayed together and shared in the chores of cooking, cleaning and gardening. Obed's idea was that discipleship was learnt through shared lives quite as much as through formal teaching. He wanted these first-generation Christians to see faith modelled close-up. Largely because of Obed's determination that it would work, it did, though not without some major hiccoughs. Dayak culture, as any other, did not readily bow to the authority and discipline of a Bible-centred lifestyle.

Prayer was central to the new college. As well as the regular staff and student prayer meetings, prayer was the first resource used to meet the challenges that arose.

To most of the new students, prayer was a formal exercise, not a personal relating with God, and Bible study was about gaining knowledge (the Indonesian education system did not relate learning to practice!) One of the biggest blessings of being on the staff was seeing the changes the Holy Spirit worked in students' lives.

The first Wednesday of the month was set aside for prayer. For many of the students this day became one of the highlights of the school programme. Bruce and Obed also suggested the concept to the national church, and it was made a policy decision in their next conference.

50

So Bruce and Annette started a long phase of their lives at SAA. At first the dramatic change from the vibrant life of Nanga Merakai was hard on everyone, including Margaret, who joined the staff as administrator, and later for Janny who joined the lecturing staff when Margaret returned home. Joan Campbell also joined the staff as a lecturer. But for Bruce, who did not take easily to change, it was the hardest. Slowly he accepted the fact that he was training a generation of pastors and church leaders, thus multiplying his ministry.

Bruce was first and foremost an evangelist. This was the gift God had given him. He had enjoyed teaching in the KKS, especially preparing the students for the weekend preaching, but had not thought of himself as a teacher. The Bible School changed that and Bruce soon realised that he had a gift of teaching also.

Bruce and Obed, along with Woodi and Janny, both gifted teachers, taught the Bible subjects. Bruce also taught evangelism and basic preaching skills. The students enjoyed his subjects because he had the ability to bring Bible truth alive through his illustrations (and his humour), and he had an amazing Bible knowledge. He was almost as at home in his Indonesian Bible as his English one.

Every second weekend, the staff and students went out on ministry to surrounding villages. Bruce could preach to his heart's content and, as almost all the villages needed gospel teaching, he did just that! Some villages were quite a trek away – so Bruce was usually given those (with the students complaining that they could not keep up with him!)

Later the senior students also gave messages, so Bruce was in his element teaching preaching skills and preparing them for ministry. Some of the Bible School-trained pastors who learnt homiletics from Bruce and Woodi could give better messages than many theology degree graduates!

The Bible School had two long holidays to fit in with the busy seasons in the rice-field. It was then that seminars and lay training courses, with evangelistic meetings in the evenings, were held in even the most remote areas of the work. In the Suruk area, before roads were built, this meant five days' boat travel up the Kapuas, Bunut and Suruk rivers.

Bruce and Annette loved this ministry and gave themselves to it with abandon. Paul and Simon, now both being home-schooled, usually joined them, bringing their school work (which they didn't do!) and enjoying the unlimited swimming, fishing, hunting and other activities that made life in Kalimantan (for boys, at least) so idyllic.

51

Beginning in 1980, evangelistic campaigns were held every few years in the five main areas of the work. For three weeks, teams of GPSK workers and missionaries were joined by a visiting team – the first being from the IMF Theological College in East Java.

As far as Bruce saw things, it was through these campaigns that there finally was a deeper, long-lasting work of God among the Dayaks in the GPSK area.

The time was ripe for the campaigns. Loggers had cut roads into the interior, making travel easier. Villages were becoming fewer and bigger. Each had a schoolroom suitable for large meetings; many had church buildings too.

During the three campaigns held during the 1980s and a fourth in 1994, about 5,500 people responded. Some had resisted the gospel for years; some were 'Christians' who had slid back into paganism or had never really understood the gospel; many were teenagers making first-time commitments.

The first campaign also resulted in students from the visiting team remaining for their 'practical' year – a wonderful help to the workers seeking to follow-up the 1,500 folk counselled. This began a regular stream of students who helped to fill the many places without full-time workers.

In December 1986 Bruce and Annette took two very reluctant sons home to Australia to stay. Many voices advised against returning to Indonesia and leaving sixteen-year-old Simon. It was a heart-wrenching time for Bruce and Annette who longed to stay with the boys until they were well settled. But the Lord's call had not changed and if they lost the visa they had miraculously kept for 20 years, there was slim hope of another.

So Bruce returned to Kalimantan, with Annette following three months later. Just before her departure in September 1987, the Lord gave them both the same promise for their boys, from Isaiah 54:13 (*'All your sons will be taught by the Lord, and great will be your children's peace'*) which in Indonesian uses the word 'disciples'. Neither of the boys were disciples at that time.

It was five years before the promise was fulfilled for Simon and another five for Paul. Meanwhile, the ache of separation was exacerbated by the lack of communication (no phones in the interior; even letters were lost.) But Bruce and Annette agreed that they learnt much more about trusting God and the power of prayer than ever before.

One day, Bruce and Annette received an urgent call to go down to Sintang. Sam's husband, Robin, had died suddenly. He was only in his early 40s and their youngest child was just 18 months old.

Bruce and Annette hurried down for the funeral and Annette stayed on for a week. After a few days, when the many relatives and friends had departed, Sam began to sort Robin's papers. She came to Annette in tears. She had found a diary he had begun before they were married.

'You'll have to read this,' she told Annette. 'I can't read it out to you.' And she wept.

Annette picked up the diary. 'Tonight I went up to see Bapak (Bruce) about marrying Samsia and he challenged me as to the reality of my relationship with Christ. I wasn't sure. I could see that he was doubtful about where I stood spiritually. On my return home I got down by my bed and made sure that I really did belong to the Lord. From this day I know I am truly His child.'

To Sam this was the most wonderful find, the confirmation that removed any doubt that lingered. Robin, although so involved in the church, had seemed to lack that 'witness of the Spirit'. Annette wept for joy with her.

52

All around the Dayaks, the scenery was shifting. Diesel generators had brought electricity and TV and thus such strange sights as American soap operas and the World Wrestling Federation.

The Suharto Government was also putting money directly into their villages. It took a few years to get this right – at first some villages spent most of it on whisky. But it began to do some real good if it did not disappear somewhere between the local government and a greedy village leader. The assistance money could be used, for example, for a village to buy a chainsaw. Other assistance money went into building bridges and improving the paths between villages.

Professional loggers and gold miners were also being given the keys to the jungle of West Kalimantan, changing it forever. Whole landscapes were stripped and cleared, in many areas replaced by lucrative palm-oil plantations. For decades, *rakit* or log-rafts had been floated lazily down the rivers to the coast. Now the logging companies produced more and bigger logs, and enormous rafts were pushed along by powerful boats to hasten the long trip, as the millennia-old jungle was slowly converted to plywood and sent to the West.

Tailings from the gold mines began to turn the acidic, black but clean Ketungau River into a filthy yellow-brown, dramatically reducing the previously abundant fish population.

Then a rush began for gold dredging, causing even the mighty Kapuas River to become clogged with islands of silt. This environmentally-destructive practice diminishes water quality and fish stocks. It causes mercury to enter the river and air and ultimately the nervous systems of animals and humans. (In the Ketungau there have already been human casualties, yet officialdom continues to look the other way.)

The wildlife retreated. Rare treasures like the clouded leopard (which even in Bruce's early days only the old people had seen) were long gone from the area. Vanishing next were the crocodiles, the orang utangs, the butterflies, the red-coated Proboscis monkeys called *hidung mancung* meaning 'long narrow nose'. (Indonesians called Westerners *hidung mancung* too, but the latter were a 'species' that was not dying out.) Gone too from the main rivers was the beautiful call of the Gibbon monkeys.

There were other tragedies along the way. Dayaks used to stun the river fish by throwing in a jungle plant called the *tuba* whose sap was a narcotic. The stunned fish rose to the surface so were easily captured and *tuba* had no ill-effects. Then someone discovered you could achieve the same results with DDT and weedkiller and do it on a large scale!

The change in education was the most dramatic. The once sleepy little town of Sintang now has its own university with 2000 students as well as over 1000 more in training for specialised fields like nursing. Work opportunities in the interior are extremely limited except for nursing or teaching, so many graduates move to the capital or even further afield. Young men often have the chance to make some money working in the palm oil industry, or in the logging trade, although most return home.

On the whole, Dayaks straddled the gap quite successfully. As road transport improved, Dayaks began to acquire motorbikes. Some enterprising people started motorbike taxi services between the villages. Bus services grew and it became quite normal for villagers to visit Sintang or even Pontianak.

So in the space of 30 years – spanning the period between Bruce and Annette's arrival in Kalimantan and the end of their ministry – there were enormous changes.

In the beginning of that time Dayaks lived in longhouses, cultivated rice, harvested rubber and ate what they grew or found in the forest or the river. They rarely travelled beyond their immediate area. By the end the people were in their own houses – almost no longhouses left except in the Iban areas. And – by far the biggest change to their lifestyle – many had TV and pirate videos.

In the villages much else remains the same. Many houses still lack amenities and most families still make their living working their rice-fields, harvesting rubber for sale, and cultivating pepper gardens. Even those in the small towns often continue to work their own land to supplement their wages.

53

What of spiritual life among the Dayaks? Well, there are lots of churches and fine Christians. Ladies' ministry and networks are a particular strength. In that sense there has been transformation. But, just as in many parts of the West, throughout the Dayak regions, the dominant note is apathy and materialism. Keen Christians can cut isolated figures in their villages. Pastors struggle. To date the TV is conquering Dayakland, not Christ.

A measure of spiritual life and vitality was the bloody Dayak uprising against the Madurese from 1996 onwards, that resulted in thousands of deaths – almost all Madurese. This conflict happened well outside the areas of the WEC-related church where there were few Madurese, but many Dayaks were affected. Dayaks had no fear of the Madurese (just the opposite), but what many did fear was their powerful *kuasa gelap* (black magic). Fetishes to protect from harm were revived in some villages and even ordered by the village head to be placed on the front door of all the houses.

When Bruce travelled to Pontianak or to Java on mission business he always found opportunities to share Christ, often one-to-one with fellow travellers, some of them high officials or Muslim clerics.

He made a trip to East Timor while it was still part of Indonesia, finding it to be as deeply entrenched in the occult as ever the Kalimantan Dayaks were – even more so. His teaching on the power of the gospel and Christ's authority made an impact on the small, struggling churches and there were some Christ-glorifying deliverances.

At one point during his weeks in East Timor a demon appeared in his room, looking like some monster from a horror film, telling him to leave.

'You never give up, do you?' was Bruce's response, 'but it's you that's going to have to leave.'

54

Bruce and Annette stayed long enough to see some lives come full circle. One time Bruce made a brief stop-off in his boat at Nanga Merakai, where he heard the old former witchdoctor Pak Serani was in the local hospital critically ill. Bruce rushed up in his old shorts – not really suitable dress for visiting. He found Serani in his hospital bed, unconscious.

The tiny Dayak had never wavered in his Christian commitment since the day he'd burnt all his idols. He was still a Dayak of the old generation: shy, self-effacing, smiling through a betel-nut-blackened mouth with most of his teeth lost in the jungle.

Taking his hand, Bruce sat with him, talking about God and his goodness. Somehow, he felt Serani was listening, and he stayed for a long time. Perhaps he reminisced about the time he'd tried to teach Serani to pray out loud. Bruce was standing waist-deep in the river beside Serani, who was in his canoe.

'I'll pray a phrase then you just pray it after me!'

'OK'

'Are you ready?'

'Yes.'

So Bruce prayed and there was a pause and Pak Serani said, laughing,

'I just can't!'

And he really couldn't, but he could chant Dayak-style a few of the Bible choruses Annette had taught him in the dialect.

Or maybe he remembered the time shortly after their return from a year in Australia. Pak Serani had caught a huge fish in the Ketungau River, wrapped it lovingly in some leaves, and smiling shyly, brought it as a present to Annette, kissing her hand with all the grace of an ambassador meeting a princess.

After a prayer committing Serani to the Lord, Bruce walked quietly down the passage toward the river. He passed the young doctor's office, and the doctor, a Muslim whom Bruce had not met, called out to him,

'*Pak Pendeta*, please drop in. I'd like to talk with you.'

Bruce protested that he was only wearing shorts but the doctor insisted, so he entered and sat down.

The doctor came immediately to the point. 'I saw you a moment ago with that patient. You love that old man, don't you? Pardon me for saying so, but I'm amazed that you, as a foreigner, could have such a close relationship with an old village man. What is the background to that?'

So Bruce recounted the whole story of Serani, from the time he had been a witchdoctor banging the drum on the veranda to drive Bruce away. When he finished, the Muslim doctor was silent for a very long time, and was still thoughtful when Bruce took his leave. A few hours later, Serani died.

55

During one of the revival campaigns, Bruce was in Nanga Merakai when his old friend Jambi came up to him.

'You know,' said Jambi, 'it's hard, once you've closely followed the Lord, and then slipped back, to start following again.'

'That's true,' said Bruce, and they fixed up a time to talk.

Jambi had a problem that is unusual in the West, though common enough elsewhere. His father, a powerful and influential witchdoctor, had died a few months earlier.

Jambi told Bruce, 'now, every time I sit down to eat a meal, my dad appears and tells me to make an offering to the ancestors. I don't know what to do.'

'Don't you remember all that I taught you?' asked Bruce after considering this. 'That's not your father at all; it's a demon deceiving you. That's what demons do – deceive and lead people astray.'

'But it looks just like my father.'

'Of course it does. Your father was so involved with the demons that they knew him well. They knew just what he looked like and how he acted.'

'So what should I do?'

'Take authority over it in Jesus' name and tell it to go away. Tell it to go wherever Jesus would send it. Tell it never to trouble you any more because you belong to Jesus, you are united with him, and you share his authority over evil forces.'

A few days later, Bruce met Jambi in the market.

'Are you having any more trouble at mealtimes?'

'No, it has never come back.'

But in all of this – preaching and teaching, leadership and fulfilment – something faded from Bruce's life towards the end of their time at Nanga Lebang.

Dayaks were still meeting Christ through Bruce's ministry, still being set free from sin and fear. Students and young pastors were being mentored and families being counselled. Although the GPSK church was fully independent, Bruce remained a consultant to the church synod and had a wide ministry.

The WEC team had shrunk from 23 in 1983 to ten in 1986, and by the early 1990s only five remained. Some lost visas, others returned home because of children's schooling. Filling the gaps in ministry were young, inexperienced Bible school graduates and some fell by the way. The responsibility of training programmes and pastoral care fell to a few.

The increased ministry load didn't faze Bruce, but there were other, more trying pressures – problems in the synod leadership, criticism, misunderstanding and lack of unity among workers. These pressures contributed to Pak Obed having a mild breakdown and it took its toll on Bruce also.

The realization slowly dawned on Bruce that he had lost something, actually the most important thing. Somewhere during this time, Bruce's first love for Jesus had cooled. His love for the Word and his passion for sharing the gospel never diminished, but there was that 'something' missing. Bruce pressed on, not really sorting it out, busy, bluff, a little sad.

HOME

56

In January 1995 WEC Indonesia added the Malay and the East Timorese to the unreached people groups they believed God wanted them to serve. Teams were forming to work among them. Bruce and Annette were asked to head up the Malay team.

For some years, Bruce and Annette had had a prayer burden for Muslims, especially the Malay peoples. The majority population of the village of Nanga Lebang across the river from them was Malay, as were most of the little townships and villages along the banks of the Kapuas River. But they had never thought of actually working among them, as direct ministry was out of the question anyway; they would have been tipped out of the country.

The request was a complete surprise, yet almost immediately they were sure that this call was of God.

The GPSK church and especially the Bible school were anything but sure! They found it very difficult to accept, not only because there were as yet no nationals to replace the Rattrays in the Bible School, but virtually none in the area of pastoral care either.

Bruce and Annette needed GSPK's blessing and it was given, very reluctantly, with the proviso that they return regularly for ministry. Bruce and Annette gladly agreed – nothing could have kept them away!

In September 1995 Bruce read something in his morning devotions that had an unusual prophetic urgency.

'This is what the LORD says: "When seventy years are completed for Babylon, I will come to you and fulfil my gracious promise to bring you back to this place.

'"For I know the plans I have for you," declares the LORD, "plans to prosper you and not to harm you, plans to give you a hope and a future."' (Jeremiah 29:10-11)

Seventy years – the Bible's way of saying the full, ripe, perfect time. And now back to the land you came from, at least for a season. *And there I will bless you.*

Bruce and Annette were still at Nanga Lebang and were not yet due for home leave. Annette, however, had been unwell and had suggested an early return. This word of scripture seemed to confirm they should leave as soon as possible.

Arriving in Brisbane in October, they had the usual health exam and all was well. A few weeks later, Bruce woke with a sense that the Holy Spirit was saying to him clearly, '*get your prostate checked*'. After the doctor's verification that there was an abnormality, he quickly organized tests and a bone scan. It was close to the Christmas holidays, so they had a further month's wait to see a specialist.

Bruce was in excellent health. The tests had found a small tumour and it was while the specialist was washing his hands that Bruce first heard the word 'cancer'.

'Oh, yeah,' the specialist said over his shoulder in response to Bruce's question. 'It's cancer alright.'

In Bruce and Annette's following newsletter, Bruce wrote,

'After the initial period of facing up to the implications of this news, there came a deep peace, even joy. Every doctor's visit, each test and its result were accompanied by that deep peace which "passes all understanding". And undergirding it all was the confidence that God was in charge, just as He had said to me before we had left Nanga Lebang. *"I know the plans that I am planning for you, plans for welfare and not calamity."* Praise Him that His plans are good and perfect.'

Radiotherapy was organized, delayed by a few months while Bruce returned to Indonesia to renew his visa. It went well and they remained at home for a further few months.

In January 1997, Bruce and Annette returned to Kalimantan for the last six months before moving into the new ministry. Bruce had no reason to believe that the cancer would trouble him. He was quite healthy.

Leaving Kalimantan meant leaving the place where most of their memories of married life were. It meant leaving their adopted families, friends and ministry of 30 years. It also meant beginning a different way of life and ministry – no more open evangelism, no more unlimited public ministry, no more living among Dayak colleagues in a familiar setting. (As of 1993, all of their colleagues in Kalimantan were nationals except for Fred and Gertrude Woodward and Myrtle Whitehead.)

Annette recalled: 'As with every major upheaval, it was a traumatic time for us, but we knew that God, not WEC, was directing us. The Word of God was alive with reminders of "all the way he had led us" – his love, protection, provision and abundant grace. Although we were nearing retirement age, we both looked forward to the challenge and privilege of sharing the Good News with those who have believed for centuries the lie that, "To be a Malay is to be a Muslim."'

So in June 1997 they left Kalimantan for the Javanese city of Malang to replace the team leader during her home leave. In the November they took a break in Australia for Simon's wedding, at which Bruce officiated, and to spend time with prayer partners.

Bruce and Annette spent a few weeks in Tasmania with their old friend Stewart Dinnen, taping many of the stories that have found their way into this book. (Stewart had passed some of the intervening years being International Director of WEC, but had now returned to Tasmania.)

In July 1998 they returned to Indonesia and moved to Sumatra. Bruce was still well, with no sign of the cancer, and he began to involve himself enthusiastically in the new ministry of encouraging and facilitating the national Christians to reach the Malays.

This changed in the December when he experienced pain while on a month's visit to West Kalimantan. Bruce took medication, but by January he was feeling increasingly unwell and the steady pain in his bones was too deep for the medicine to reach. He perspired so profusely that Annette would wring the water out of the towels on his mattress each morning. He was excessively tired.

Each new week seemed to bring a fresh depth of trial. Finally, Bruce said, 'Sweetheart, you've got to get me home.' It was February and a mini-conference of their small team was planned for the following week. As the leaders, they had felt they should stay. Annette quickly organized flights and for the first time in their lives together, she humped the luggage while all Bruce could do was sit and watch, or sometimes lie down and sleep.

Back in Brisbane, the oncologist diagnosed a spectacular advance of the prostate cancer into the bones. He gave Bruce a new treatment, a three-monthly implant which sent the cancer symptoms into an almost equally dramatic reversal. Within a few months Bruce felt well and ready to go again, though the old enormous strength and vitality was gone forever.

Bruce and Annette returned to Indonesia in June 2000 for a final stint – the first few weeks in Kalimantan followed by five months in Malang, East Java.

The implant was only a temporary relief though, not a cure, and towards the end of their time in Malang the blood test showed the all-telling PSA count had risen. Bruce also recognized the returning symptoms. In November 2000, they returned home.

Following the specialist's report, Bruce wrote, 'The doctor confirmed that the implant was losing its effectiveness. Although there were a few things that they could try to address this, the present trend will continue unless the Lord sovereignly intervenes.' Bruce had no doubt that he could.

57

Bruce was often asked about healing. He was known as a man of faith. Had he asked for healing? He had seen God do miracles and healings through him, so why not for him? Why hadn't he claimed it?

Bruce's reply was always the same – an evidence of his settled assurance of God's loving and sovereign purposes, the 'good and perfect' plans for him.

'I know that God can heal me, and if it is his will to do so, he will give me the faith to claim healing. I just want his will, whether I am healed or not.'

At times Bruce would be facetious, as he was wont to be, and shock enquirers by saying, 'Oh, I don't bother God about such things!' It was his way of saying that he had no quarrel with the one he knew and loved so well.

Still the cancer advanced as did the steady pain and the tiredness. In July 2001 he had an already long-planned hip replacement to help regain some mobility.

The Australian winter turned to spring, and Bruce realized that even with a new hip he wasn't going to walk too many more steps in his life. Almost the last act was a meeting with the oncologist in October 2001 that revealed an extremely high PSA count and finally removed all medical hope of a further remission.

So what of God's plans for 'welfare and not calamity' spoken to Bruce and Annette in September 1995? Did they still believe his plans were 'good and perfect'? Did they still believe that he was 'making their way perfect'? They certainly did.

This did not alter the reality of the depth of suffering, or of the heartache at seeing their loved ones, especially their sons, suffer with them. And it was a long and painful 'way'.

But more of a reality was the assurance that it was his perfect way for them. And the deep peace Bruce had spoken of at the very beginning did not change even through the darkest times.

On different occasions Bruce and Annette had taken their sons aside and apologized for their failings as parents, which they felt were very great.

Their sons seemed to harbour no regrets for having a father who was away on ministry for much of their early years. They were and remain proud of him and would not have chosen a different upbringing, or for Mum and Dad to have had different priorities.

Paul adds, 'Between my being away at boarding school, hunting or fishing, and Dad away or busy, the limited time he did spend with me was a valuable learning experience.

'Dad taught me to be competitive and strive to do my best at whatever I set out to do. Mum and Dad's love and respect for the Dayaks also rubbed off on me. Because they allowed me to spend much of my time with the local people, I learnt to speak their language fluently, and developed cultural and bush skills that I still have to this day.'

Simon recalls: 'It was not until after Dad died that I began to truly appreciate the immense power of his prayer life. The day he died, I felt a foreboding sense of weakness and isolation. It was as if a mantle of protection had left me and I was now exposed to the spiritual elements.

'All through my life, Dad's prayers had protected me and

comforted me, and they had quickened me – I have no doubt his prayers even moved me to repentance. I am sure his prayers are still being answered today. I don't think I have yet or ever will really understand this awesome mechanic of prayer, but I am thankful that a glimpse of it was modelled for me in my father.'

Following the last meeting with the oncologist, Bruce wrote, 'We are so blessed to be in the family of God. Thank you for your prayers and loving support of us. Pray with us that, as these are part of the good works ordained for us (Ephesians 2:10), we will walk in them to his glory.'

He signed it as follows:

Garrisoned by his peace,
Bruce (and Annette)

EPILOGUE

Glenn Myers

I met the Rattrays in November 2001. Annette found me at the airport, where I had stood waiting in the sunlight just long enough – a few minutes – to wonder if it was indeed Brisbane I was supposed to fly to, and not, say, Adelaide or Perth.

I was hopefully eyeing up various elderly Australian women in the airport lounge when Annette greeted me. Annette turned out to be petite, warm-hearted, strong-minded, hard-working and with rather scary driving habits. (In Annette's case, after most of their 30 years in the jungle rarely seeing a car, she had only returned to driving since Bruce had relinquished the wheel some months before.)

She took me to their home in the suburbs of Brisbane. There was a smoke-blue jacaranda tree in full bloom outside their house, and two parrots in a cage on their bougainvillea-clad balcony. Bruce was installed in an armchair, his leg in a white stocking that gave him a rather Shakespearian look. He had a big, lived-in face, grey-green eyes, white hair, and mottled skin that now hung like a curtain around his huge frame. He looked much older than his 68 years, and merriment was spilling out of him. Though he was in a great deal of pain, I found him relaxed, happy, full of fun.

For the next three weeks, not leaving the room, we went on trek together.

Late in my stay I asked him about the cancer. He talked about some dark times: the first diagnosis, and losing the strength and physical invulnerability that he had enjoyed all his life. A long respite, then a second dark time as the implant stopped working and the cancer crept back.

Finally, trying to recover from the hip operation and the realization that he wasn't going to get better. In all of this he had to watch Annette suffer with him.

Then he turned to what for him was the important side, the spiritual side.

He explained, 'I've had a lot of people praying for me – prayer partners, fellow missionaries, a lot of national believers. I remember one lady used to get out of bed at night and pray specifically for me. I think I would put a lot of it down to prayer.

'I'm not aware that I've done anything. All I know is that little by little, over that dark period, the Lord has given light.

'But the thing that is most blessed of all for me is, that deep abiding love for the Lord Jesus, that always was there, was back again – fresh. Yeah. I felt the Lord broke me up all over again, I'd have to say almost sovereignly – and in a way that didn't hurt very much. Just that I became deeply aware of it, and then little by little, it happened.

'And I've said many times: I know that I am much better, a much better man of God, since the cancer than I was before.

'So nowadays, a good day is without any pain, I take that as a bonus. A good sleep of a night, without any pain – I just ... I don't sing much any more (I don't have any voice anyway) but sometimes I can hardly contain myself from singing.

'What does it say? *"He gives me songs in the night."* Yeah, I know what that means. There were songs rising in my heart, brother. That's the greatest thing of all. I can lie in my bed at night. And I want to spring forth with praise. I just lie there, if awake, thinking about the goodness of the Lord and his love for me.'

Our interviews were often halted by visits and phone calls – former missionaries, family members, people the Rattrays' lives had touched, members of the church into which they'd settled in Brisbane.

I don't know if the callers were expecting to find a dying man and a grieving wife. What they were finding (I was finding it myself) was a couple who were overflowing with interest in you and love for God – wise, warm, welcoming. You seemed to leave their house with a lot more than you arrived with.

I visited their church, saw the respect and love a young fellowship had for these seasoned Christian workers. Bruce didn't preach, though he wasn't beyond calling out encouragement to the pastor mid-sermon. He had actually spoken in public for the final time just a couple of weeks previously, a simple testimony to answer a question posed by the senior pastor: Was it worth it?

In January, there was a reunion of Kalimantan missionaries near Brisbane. Bruce was too sick to attend, but ex-colleagues from as far as Holland and Alaska came for a visit and to say goodbye. It was an emotional time of reminiscing and thanksgiving, but with lots of laughter too. (The ranks had recently been thinned, however: Bruce's meticulous colleague, Woodi, had counted

15 West Kalimantan missionaries who had developed cancer; Woodi himself died of a cancerous condition the month before the reunion.)

Soon after this, Bruce began to deteriorate, suffering increasingly severe pain. On February 16 he became paralysed from the waist down and suffered a mild stroke, both caused by the cancer. The following day he was hospitalised, lapsed into a coma and was not expected to live through the night. The next morning, he rallied, causing the doctor (not a Christian) to say, 'He did a Lazarus on us!'

Bruce's last three days were a gracious 'extra', as he was relatively pain-free, was able to talk, though with difficulty, sharing his testimony and even joking with an amazed staff. Phone calls brought their far-flung family and friends close and he continually spoke of heaven. His oft-repeated remark was, 'I have one foot in heaven and can't wait for the other to follow!' He was longing to meet the Lord and Saviour he loved.

His last words on 21 February 2002, very haltingly spoken, were, 'Life has no meaning without Jesus Christ.'

GLOSSARY

Indonesian and Dayak words used in the text:

Asal sembuh	'... so long as they get better!' (we'll try anything)
Belantik	bamboo spear sprung as a trap for wild pigs
Bram/beram	rice wine
Dukun	occult spirit practitioner or spirit healer
Jalan Tuhan	the Lord's way
Gawai	feast
Hidung mancung	Proboscis monkey (also sometimes 'Westerner')
Jayau	magic spell
Ketua adat	cultural head of an area, who presides over all traditions and judges disputes
Kuasa gelap	black magic
Kuli	labourer
Kristen Protestan	Protestant Christian, one of the five legal religions of Indonesia
Masuk jalan Tuhan	'enter the Lord's way' (start to follow the Christian path)
Manang	'priest', witchdoctor, person in charge of village rituals
Naneng	very large wasp or hornet
Nanga	mouth of river
Pantang	taboo

Pak / Bapak	Mr, Sir, Father
Pendeta	minister of religion
Penumpang	passengers
Rakit	log rafts
Surau	Muslim prayer house
Tuan	'white man'
Tuba	root of jungle plant with narcotic properties
Utusan Injil	*Gospel Messenger* (name of one of the mission boats)

MAPS

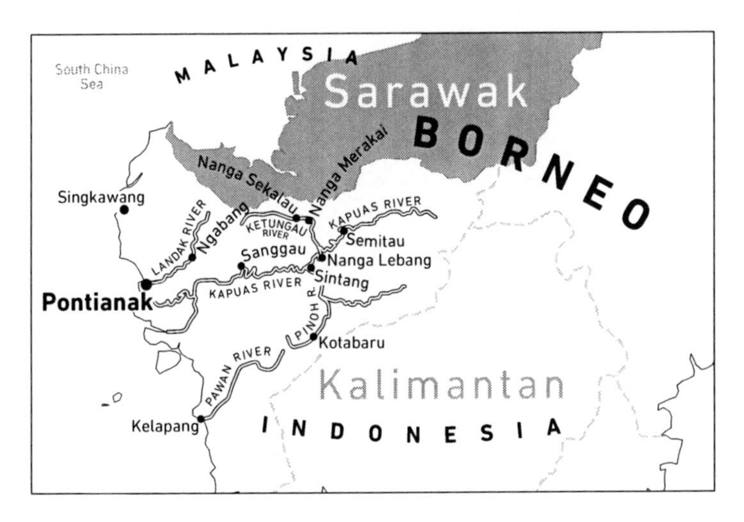
South China Sea
MALAYSIA
Sarawak
BORNEO
Nanga Merakai
Nanga Sekalau
Singkawang
LANDAK RIVER
Ngabang
KETUNGAU RIVER
KAPUAS RIVER
Semitau
Sanggau
Nanga Lebang
Sintang
Pontianak
KAPUAS RIVER
PINOH R.
Kotabaru
PAWAN RIVER
Kalimantan
Kelapang
INDONESIA

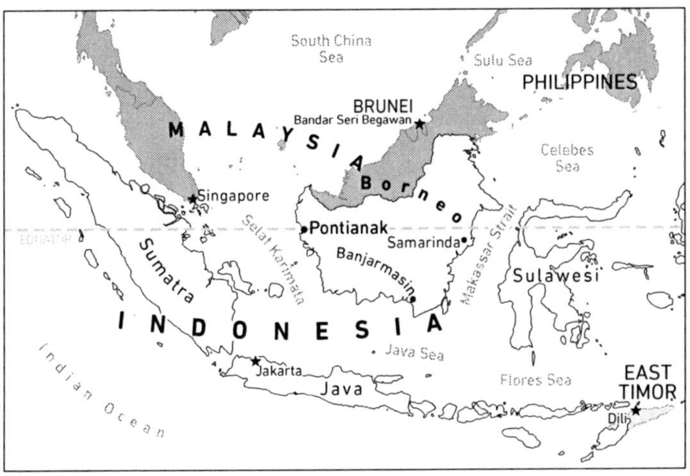
South China Sea
Sulu Sea
PHILIPPINES
BRUNEI
Bandar Seri Begawan
MALAYSIA
Celebes Sea
Borneo
Singapore
Selat Karimata
Pontianak
Samarinda
Makassar Strait
Sumatra
Banjarmasin
Sulawesi
INDONESIA
Java Sea
Indian Ocean
Jakarta
Java
Flores Sea
EAST TIMOR
Dili

ABOUT WEC

WEC International is a mission agency with over 1800 workers drawn from 50 countries serving in multicultural teams among nearly 100 unreached peoples of the world. From its beginnings in the Congo in 1913 it has grown to work in many different parts of the world. Evangelical and inter-denominational in outlook, WEC's ethos is based on four Pillars of Faith, Sacrifice, Holiness, and Fellowship. WEC's commission is to:

- bring the gospel of our Lord Jesus Christ to the remaining unevangelised peoples of the world with utmost urgency
- demonstrate the compassion of Christ to a needy world, to plant churches and lead them to spiritual maturity
- inspire, mobilise and train for cross-cultural mission.

To help us achieve that, we have 16 Sending Bases scattered throughout the world which recruit, screen, send and help support workers. We also train missionary workers at six training institutes around the world.

WEC workers are involved in almost every type of direct outreach and support ministry related to the fulfilment of these aims. WEC's ministries range from the production of the prayer handbook *Operation World*, through the planting and establishment of churches, to helping indigenous missionary sending agencies in mature WEC fields.

WECs lifestyle

- We fervently desire to see Christ formed in us so that we live holy lives.
- In dependence on the Holy Spirit we determine to obey our Lord whatever the cost.
- We trust God completely to meet every need and challenge we face in His service.
- We are committed to oneness, fellowship and the care of our whole missionary family.

WECs convictions:

- We are convinced that prayer is a priority.
- We uphold biblical truth and standards.
- We affirm our love for Christ's Church, and endeavour to work in fellowship with local and national churches, and with other Christian agencies.
- We accept each other irrespective of gender, ethnic background or church affiliation.
- We desire to work in multi-national teams and are committed to effective international cooperation.
- We recognise the importance of research and responding to God's directions for advance.
- We believe in full participation and oneness in decision making.
- We value servant leaders who wait on God for vision and direction.
- We promote local and innovative strategies through decentralised decision making.
- We make no appeals for funds.

"If Jesus Christ be God and died for me, no sacrifice can be too great for me to make for Him." **C T Studd, founder of WEC**

Visit **www.wec-int.org** for more information.

Lightning Source UK Ltd.
Milton Keynes UK
28 April 2010

153490UK00001B/26/P